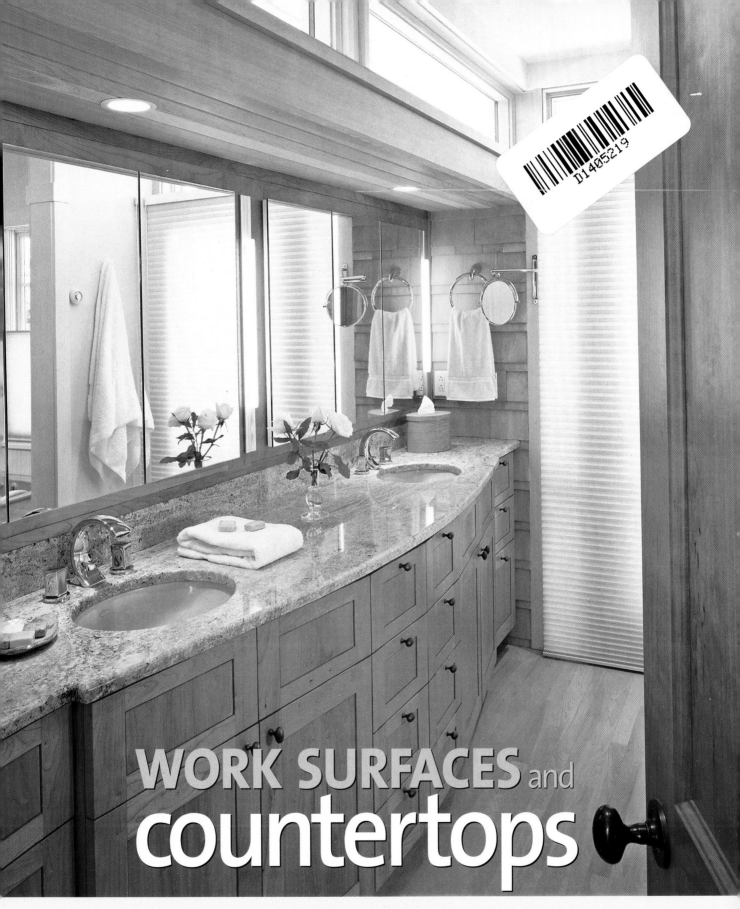

WORK SURFACES and
countertops

By Lisa Stockwell Kessler and the Editors of Sunset Books

MENLO PARK, CALIFORNIA

SUNSET BOOKS

VP, GENERAL MANAGER:
Richard A. Smeby
VP, EDITORIAL DIRECTOR:
Bob Doyle
PRODUCTION DIRECTOR:
Lory Day
OPERATIONS DIRECTOR:
Rosann Sutherland
MARKETING MANAGER:
Linda Barker
EXECUTIVE EDITOR:
Bridget Biscotti Bradley
ART DIRECTOR:
Vasken Guiragossian
SPECIAL SALES:
Brad Moses

STAFF FOR THIS BOOK

WRITER:
Lisa Stockwell Kessler
MANAGING EDITOR:
Marianne Lipanovich
CONTRIBUTING EDITOR:
Scott Atkinson
COPY EDITOR:
Carol Whiteley
ART DIRECTOR:
Vasken Guiragossian
ILLUSTRATOR:
Rik Olson
PAGE PRODUCTION:
Janie Farn
PREPRESS COORDINATOR:
Eligio Hernandez
INDEXER:
Barbara J. Braasch
PROOFREADERS:
Joan Beth Erickson
Michelle Pollace

Cover main image: photography by
Todd Caverly. Bottom left: photography
by Muffy Kibbey. Bottom middle:
photography by E. Andrew McKinney.
Bottom right: photography by Thomas
J. Story.

For their assistance on this book,
we'd like to thank Surface Art,
Healdsburg, CA 95448. We'd also
like to thank Beverley Bozarth
Colgan and Anthony Davis for additional illustrations.

10 9 8 7 6 5 4 3 2 1

First Printing June 2005

For additional copies of *Work Surfaces and Countertops* or any other Sunset book,
call 1-800-526-5111 or visit us at www.sunset.com.

contents

counter culture

A countertop or work surface is one of the most functional elements in any working room in your home. Your choice of materials will make it either a focal point of the room or an area that blends into the background. A well-designed countertop can help set a style, from ultramodern to traditional to rustic, and add character to your space. And if it's maintained and cared for, it will serve you well for many years.

Countertops can be created from almost any hard material you can imagine. Today's choices include synthetics, ceramic tiles, metal, wood, and stone. Not every material is appropriate for every situation. In this chapter, we discuss the factors that will influence your selection. Your decision will depend on what the surface will be used for, your design preferences, the style of your home, your budget, and how much work you're willing to do to maintain the surface.

Before you choose a material or color, consider all your options. You'll find a comprehensive review of each one in the next chapter. Then pick the combination that best suits your needs.

A sloped dish drainer built into an engineered-stone countertop lets you do away with bulky dish racks.

getting started

Some work surface materials can be used just about anywhere. Others are fine for some purposes, but can be a poor choice for a specific location or activity. To ensure that the material you select is appropriate, consider where you want to put it and which tasks will be performed on it.

SUITING THE FUNCTION

The most challenging room to outfit with work surfaces is the kitchen, because you perform many different tasks there—everything from chopping vegetables to rolling dough to drying dishes to writing shopping lists. Traditionally, homeowners have chosen a single material for this space, but no one surface is perfect for every job. Today, you can easily mix materials, using a different one for each workstation. For example, use a butcher block for a cutting and chopping area,

marble for a pastry and bread-making station, and heat-resistant natural stone and ceramic tile next to the stove. If you'd like to use just one material, you can supplement it with task-specific kitchen tools, such as cutting and pastry boards, heatproof trivets, and dish racks.

In the bathroom, a countertop is used primarily for storage and should be flat and smooth. Because bath items such as toothpaste, soap, bath oil, and makeup can leave marks, your best choice is a water- and stain-resistant surface that is easy to clean.

Work surfaces in home offices, laundry and hobby rooms, patios, and garden sheds all serve a single purpose, so materials for these countertops should be chosen accordingly. An office work area should be smooth and hard so that it provides a good writing surface. Laundry countertops need to be smooth so they won't

snag clothing. Surfaces designed for sewing rooms and playrooms should be impervious to scissors, markers, and crayons. Outdoor surfaces should be weatherproof and water resistant.

And nearly all work surfaces everywhere need to be able to withstand the occasional dropped object, spill, and pounding.

MAINTAINING THE TOP

Countertop materials fall into two categories: those that retain their original color and texture over time with only minimal maintenance, and those that take on a new patina with age. Materials that are not naturally stain, heat, and scratch resistant can be kept in their original condition with regular sealing, waxing, or sanding. If you don't like the aged look or want that extra work, invest in one of the low-maintenance options.

However, if you're attracted to a material that may change appearance with continuous use, ask the supplier for a sample square you can test before you make your purchase. If the surface will be used in the kitchen, for example, rub it with ingredients it would come in contact with, then wipe the sample clean and observe the result.

Two contrasting colors of stone—white marble and honed charcoal limestone—break up the large center island with a sensuous curving pattern.

design considerations

The best work surface for your space is the one that appeals to your taste and suits your budget. But to create the most attractive presentation in any room, it's important that the countertop work together with other design elements in the room. You are the best judge of what you like and the type of environment that makes you comfortable, but two major guidelines can help you narrow down your choices. The first is to consider and suit the architectural style of your home. The second is to understand the effects color and

texture have on a design scheme and how to work with them most effectively.

SUITING THE STYLE

Whether you live in an authentic period home or one with no obvious history, you can look to architectural style for inspiration in selecting a work surface material. The most common architectural styles in the U.S. are Colonial, Neo-Classical, Victorian, Mediterranean, Arts and Crafts, rustic, and contemporary.

To stay true to a specific style, select materials that were available to the builders of that period. For instance, countertops in traditional English and Colonial homes were most often made of

LEFT: A textured laminate top with metal edging is the perfect solution for this 1950s retro kitchen.

A white solid surface material and light butcher block blend into the background of this country kitchen and let the colorful stenciling dominate.

TOP LEFT: A natural stone countertop always complements traditional wood cabinetry. A semi-circular extension beyond the sink adds a modern touch.

RIGHT: Attention to detail is the hallmark of the Arts and Crafts style, here demonstrated by the design inlay in this solid surface countertop.

ABOVE: A kitchen instantly takes on Mexican Colonial style with blue and white ceramic tile.

BOTTOM LEFT: The Art Deco–style bathroom is enhanced by a pink marble vanity top.

wood. In Tuscany homes, builders used limestone and light-colored marble. In Spain and Mexico, ceramic tile was the popular choice. Beginning in the middle of the 20th century, man-made materials were not only popular, they became more cost effective than their natural counterparts. The look was streamlined and without texture or decorative detailing; solid-color plastic lami-nate with metal edging defined the 1950s, with more expensive stainless steel countertops in some modern homes. Self-edged or wood-edged plastic laminate was considered the most modern material for kitchen and bathroom countertops in the 1960s, and it became the low-cost option from that period on.

Since the 1980s, designers have both revived and reinterpreted traditional styles and regional designs, putting the focus back on wood, stone, and metal. Today the newest composites imitate the look of natural materials, giving homeowners the opportunity to use a low-maintenance version of the real thing. The less expensive plastic laminates also do a credible job of mimicking nature, as well as providing an extensive range of colors and unusual textures.

MIXING AND MATCHING

Interior design today is playful and eclectic, letting you mix and match materials as well as counter heights and shapes. With good engineering you can run stone, metal, wood, and composite materials side by side, or cantilever one material off another. And you're no longer limited to straight edges—curvilinear shapes can add a distinctive touch. Just be aware that, if you're not an accomplished do-it-yourselfer, the more complex the installation, the more expensive it will be.

TOP: Opaque glass "floats" over a wood countertop, one of several materials used in this eclectic kitchen.

BELOW: Because of its transparency, clear glass normally found in more contemporary designs complements the traditional styling of this white kitchen.

CHOOSING THE COLOR

If you are adding a work surface to a room with an existing color scheme, you can match one of the colors, use a contrasting color, or stick with a neutral black or white.

Black and white, considered "non-colors," play an important role in decorating because they can work alone or provide visual relief to a particular color scheme—without altering the color relationships. White reflects light and will make a space feel more open and airy. It's the most popular choice for kitchen countertops because it looks clean and never goes out of style. Black is graphic and sophisticated, and can contrast sharply with white walls as well as tone down bright colors such as red and yellow. However, it can also be austere.

If you want to add drama to a room, a colorful work surface can be an attractive way to do it. But before you select a color, it's helpful to know its effects. The color wheel is a universal design tool that aids in understanding the relationships among colors.

On the color wheel, the three pure, primary colors—red, yellow, and blue—are placed equidistant from one another. Between them are the three secondary colors—orange, green, and purple; these result from mixing equal amounts of two of the primary colors. Between the

White is one of the most popular monochromatic schemes for a kitchen. The white tile used in this island top will never go out of style.

primary and secondary colors are the tertiary colors, each formed by mixing the primary and secondary colors that flank it.

All the colors on the wheel are pure, highly saturated, and undiluted, so they are very strong for home decor. To get milder hues for your interiors, you can add either white or black to any of them.

Consider the tried-and-true methods for combining colors that follow on the next pages to select a work surface that will work with the rest of the room.

TERTIARY COLOR

PRIMARY COLOR

SECONDARY COLOR

MONOCHROMATIC COLOR SCHEMES

A monochromatic scheme may consist of a single color or different values of the same color, with the work surface either lighter or darker than the walls. If you use one of the cool colors—blue, green, or violet—a monochromatic scheme will make the room seem larger and more open. Using a warm color—red, yellow, or orange—can make a large room feel smaller or add energy to an otherwise dark room. Neutral tones, such as off-whites, creams, and grays, create a sense of understated elegance.

ANALOGOUS COLOR SCHEMES

Another way to create a harmonious effect is to combine two or more colors that are adjacent to each other on the wheel, such as jade (blue-green) and blue or yellow and marigold (yellow-orange). You can mix and match values of adjacent colors for interesting effects.

TOP: This multiple-color scheme is strong enough to support a color-flecked laminate countertop. No one element overpowers another.

RIGHT: Shades of green mosaic tiles, highlighted with touches of color, create an harmonious effect in a small bathroom.

COMPLEMENTARY COLOR SCHEMES

Colors that are directly opposite each other on the color wheel are considered complementary colors. When paired, complementary colors create a dynamic scheme, with each color appearing to gain vibrancy. If you choose this type of scheme, keep in mind that the colors usually work best if you alter their values. For instance, try a deep slate-blue countertop against a light terra-cotta wall, or a soft-pink marble top against a forest-green background. Because complementary color schemes have so much energy, you may prefer to limit them to active areas, such as the kitchen or a child's playroom. And remember that the bright colors popular today might look dated in years to come.

MULTIPLE-COLOR SCHEMES You can group three different colors successfully if they are equidistant from one another on the wheel. This kind of scheme may take the form of one color on the wall, another on cabinetry, and a third on the work surface.

TOP RIGHT: The complementary orange and blue color scheme is softened by yellow walls.

BOTTOM RIGHT: Complex color schemes can be unsettling. Adding small amounts of a third color, such as the red in this backsplash and edging, keeps the room in balance.

NEUTRALS While white and black are the true neutrals, there are other subtle colors called neutrals that actually have some color mixed into their white base. For example, if you take green to its lowest intensity, the result is a neutral. Yellow becomes a buttery off-white. Because these neutrals never overwhelm a room they are a popular choice for work surfaces. But remember that because they aren't colorless, you will need to match their hues to other colors in the room.

TOP: Gray is the dominant color in this neutral scheme, with white and black used in supporting roles.

RIGHT: A soft yellow vanity top and two mirror frames add a hint of color to an all-white bathroom.

WHICH TYPE OF TEXTURE?

There are two types of texture: "actual" and "visual." Actual texture is something you can feel, such as a rough slate surface or grout lines in a ceramic-tile countertop. Visual texture refers to patterns that appear to the eye as texture but are not, such as faux wood grain or a granite-like pattern that is stamped on plastic laminate. Such patterns imply light and shadow, creating the illusion of dimension.

Actual texture modulates color in powerful ways. Its tiny peaks and valleys absorb rather than reflect light, lowering the intensity of any color. Smooth, shiny surfaces, because they have no real texture, reflect light best and enhance a color's intensity.

Combining textures is a balancing act. Too little texture gives a room a flat, dull appearance, but too much is visually confusing. In a neutral or monochromatic scheme, be sure to combine several different textures for visual interest. In a kitchen you might mix a butcher block–topped island with a limestone countertop and stainless steel appliances.

When you're working with a more complex color scheme, unite it by using similar textures, for example, a polished blue concrete work surface and smooth yellow walls.

The rough texture of flamed granite tiles adds interest to a neutral bathroom. This surface is not recommended for work areas where smoothness is desired.

A one-of-a-kind metal backsplash and edging tiles combine with a ceramic countertop for a mix of traditional and contemporary styles.

supports and surroundings

There are several issues you need to decide on before you select a work surface material and install it: what will support it, whether or not it will need a backsplash, and how it will be edged.

BASES

The most important aspect of any base is that it supports the weight of the work surface. If a base does not provide continuous support along the length and width of the countertop, the countertop material may need special attention.

As you choose your base, remember to consider the finished height of the work surface. Some materials will add several inches to the height of the base, which can be a problem if you're installing a countertop on a wall below a window or other obstruction. Following are the most common base options for the different rooms in your home.

KITCHEN BASES The standard, most practical option for a kitchen countertop is cabinetry, with or without doors or drawers. However, while most commercial cabinets are constructed to accommodate any material, regardless of its weight, special support may be required for stone or concrete slabs that span the distance over a dishwasher or cantilever off an island or a peninsula.

You can also install a work surface on top of a rolling cart, or span it across two sets of wire-mesh drawers. Cylindrical metal or carved wood table legs or stone side panels make attractive and effective countertop supports. If you have an old table, you can set a new work surface directly on top of it, bringing the edges down far enough to hide the existing surface.

RIGHT: A chrome base on wheels allows you to move this butcher-block work surface wherever it is needed. (See page 82 for an inexpensive island you can build yourself.)

BELOW: Glass block makes an unusual but artistic base for a bathroom vanity and makeup table.

RIGHT: A wooden base, mounted on the wall, creates a streamlined design and ample undercounter storage in this contemporary Asian-inspired bathroom.

BATHROOM BASES The bathroom is a great place to be creative with a countertop base, because it is a relatively small room where a small detail can make a big statement. Cabinets are still the most popular and economical choice for a vanity base, but don't feel limited to stock bathroom-base cabinets. Kitchen-base cabinets are typically several inches taller than bathroom cabinets and create a more comfortable height for tall members of the household. For an interesting visual effect, you can raise bathroom cabinets off the floor with legs or mount them on the wall.

For an antique look, use carved wood table legs and a wood skirt to support the vanity counter. Or look for an old wood washstand or potting bench at an antique store. For a high-tech look, mount the vanity top directly on the wall or set it on top of a stainless steel frame or legs.

LEFT: In a modern bathroom, a stainless steel industrial kitchen base supports an oval granite vanity top.

ABOVE: Sawhorse legs serve as island bases in this casual Southwestern kitchen.

19

WORK AND GARDEN ROOM BASES

Table legs, file cabinets, old kitchen-base cabinets, sawhorses, tool chests, wire-mesh basket frames, and even tall clay chimney flues make effective bases for desks and worktables. Potting benches require weather-resistant materials like wood or metal legs.

Desk legs can be made from wide wood dowels as well as metal cylinders. One of the greatest innovations for the desktop is the telescoping leg, which lets you adjust the height of the desk. You can also suspend the desktop from the wall using a strong metal chain or wall brackets. Generally you should use something that provides ample legroom below any work surface you plan to sit at.

TOP: Redwood and Douglas fir are the woods of choice for outdoor bases. See page 102 for a planting table you can build yourself.

RIGHT: An open wooden base provides easy access to large baskets and vases at this flower-arranging worktable.

BACKSPLASHES

A backsplash protects the wall just above the work surface as well as prevents water, food, and small items from slipping through the crack where the countertop meets the wall. Some manufactured materials can be fabricated to include a one-piece cove backsplash with the countertop; natural materials require a two-piece construction. In this type of construction, a length of material or series of tiles, commonly 4 inches high, is installed after the countertop is in place. With many materials you can put your edging detail on top of the backsplash for an integrated look.

TOP: Plain tiles are separated by tile edging strips to create a backsplash that mimics the inlay design at the front of the solid surface countertop.

MIDDLE RIGHT: Checkerboard tiles, such as those used in this backsplash, draw the eye up from the countertop. More expensive decorative tiles are used sparingly on the wall above.

BOTTOM RIGHT: A granite backsplash is stepped down at a side wall to meet the front of the countertop.

LEFT: Honed granite looks more natural in a rustic kitchen when its edges are left jagged.

TOP: Stainless steel tiles create a backsplash behind the stove that reflects light and is easy to clean.

A two-piece squared backsplash can be made either from the same material used to make your countertop or from a complementary one. For example, you can match white ceramic tiles with natural stone or plastic laminate for a clean, uncluttered look. A decorative backsplash can give life to a simple countertop. Use multicolor ceramic or glass tiles to create a dramatic backsplash for a solid-color laminate countertop. Cover an entire wall above an inexpensive ceramic countertop with hand-painted tiles. Or use stainless steel or copper tiles to add interesting contrast to stone. When you mix and match, always consider the color and texture of all the materials used in the room.

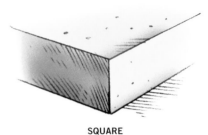

SQUARE

LEFT: Decorative curves soften the corners of a marble work island.
BELOW: The design cut into the corners of this island is repeated along the sides to add style and soften the edges.

EDGING

Once you've determined which material you will use for your work surface, you need to select an edging detail to finish off all visible edges; the one you select will affect both the style and the price of the top. An edge typically overhangs the top of the work surface by 1 inch, but some materials look better with a deeper edge. Whatever size edge you use, make sure it doesn't obstruct base drawers or doors. The most common self-edge options include square, bullnose, waterfall, bevel, and ogee. A band of wood or stainless steel can be used to edge both plastic laminate and tile.

The rounded bullnose, waterfall, and ogee edges are easiest on the eye and body. The waterfall detail may also be defined as a half-bullnose. Square edges are usually less expensive, but if you run directly into them they can cause some mean scratches or bruises. With some materials, square edges are more likely to chip.

Wood edges can be milled into any shape to match other architectural trim in the room. If you are edging tile with wood, use an epoxy grout for a stronger bond. If the grout loosens, dirt and debris will collect in the crack.

DOUBLE BEVEL

FULL BULLNOSE

WATERFALL OR HALF BULLNOSE

DOUBLE OGEE WITH BULLNOSE OFFSET

DOUBLE OGEE

the materials

There are so many options for work surfaces that no single store carries them all. If you enjoy shopping, you can go from store to store for a firsthand look at the full range of materials. But you may want to narrow down your choices before you hit the pavement.

This chapter covers every material that's suitable for a work surface. We include descriptions, costs, pros and cons, and the amount of time it will take, after ordering, to receive a fabricated countertop. The materials are listed in order of cost, from the least expensive to the most, making it easy to identify those that fit your budget.

While this primer is limited to new materials, you can make innovative and inexpensive work surfaces using recycled materials you find at salvage yards, antique shops, or yard sales. Plywood construction remnants or old hardwood boards can be pieced together and waxed or varnished to create counter or desktops. Flat doors make ideal desks or hobby tables. And old plastic laminate kitchen counters can be reused as laundry counters in a garage. If you feel especially crafty, consider purchasing old ceramic dishware, breaking it into pieces, and creating a mosaic surface on a length of fiberboard or plywood.

options at a glance

I f a material is hard and flat, it's appropriate for a work surface. But different materials have inherent characteristics that make them better for certain functions than others. The chart on the following page outlines the primary advantages and disadvantages of each material, as well as the installation costs and time frames for fabrication. Materials are listed in order of cost, from the least expensive option to the most.

TOP: *Brightly speckled laminate vanity counters are festive as well as easy to clean.*

ABOVE: *A colored concrete counter looks natural in a tile bathroom.*

LEFT: *Pastel tiles are laid in a mosaic pattern to add visual texture to neutral colored cabinets.*

MATERIAL	PROS	CONS	COST/SQ.FT. INSTALLED*	ORDER TIME
Ceramic Tile	Durable; heat resistant; many colors and patterns; several finishes	Uneven surface; grout needs to be sealed and can stain; can chip or crack	$11–$100	Varies by manufacturer
Stone Tile	Durable; natural; unlimited colors; inexpensive alternative to stone slab	Grout joints need to be sealed; limited edging options; can scratch	$11–$30	Allow 1 week to have edges bullnosed
Plastic Laminate	Inexpensive; lots of colors, patterns, and textures; easy to clean and maintain; stain resistant	Visible seams; heat will damage; burns, stains, and deep scratches can't be repaired	$15–$80	1–2 weeks
Wood	Natural; scratches and stains can be sanded; heat bars can be installed; hardwoods good for cutting	Some woods not water resistant; needs regular cleaning and sealing or waxing; limited heat resistance	$10–$200	1–6 weeks for butcher block; 4–5 weeks for solid wood tops
Richlite	Natural look like wood; develops natural patina with age; 7 colors; can span above-average lengths without support; heat resistant to 350°	Needs sealing for stain resistance; limited colors; UV rays will darken colors; limited repairability	$50–$80	3–4 weeks
Solid Surface	Nonporous; stain resistant, easy to clean; scratches and burns can be sanded; seamless; integral or undermounted sink	Extremely hot items can damage surface; can look artificial	$50–$110 undermounted or integral sink and upgraded edges are extra	7–10 working days
Metal	Durable; bacteria, heat, and stain resistant; integral sink and drainboard capability	Cold and noisy; will scratch; shows water and grease marks if not cleaned and dried properly	$60–$160	3–8 weeks
Engineered Stone	Strong; scratch, stain, and heat resistant; no need for sealing	Expensive	$60–$130	4 weeks
Natural Stone	Natural; long lasting; won't go out of style; heat- and water-proof; can be cut for under-mounted sink	Needs to be sealed for stain resistance; lime and acid etch marble; slate is most stain resistant	$70–$200	4 weeks
Concrete	Natural; many colors; heat resistant; can customize with embedded objects; integral sink and drainboard capability; smooth	Can develop cracks; needs to be sealed and sealer can be damaged by heat and knives; hard to find experienced fabricators	$75–$100	6–8 weeks
Glass	Heatproof; smooth; easy to maintain; can be painted, etched, or sandblasted	Can scratch; leaves watermarks if not towel-dried	$75–$150	1–3 weeks

*Installation costs will vary depending on the grade of material you use and the installer's rate.

ceramic tile

- Installed Price: **$11–$100 per square foot**
- Edging Options: **Bullnose, V-cap, decorative trim tiles and borders, self-edging, wood trim**
- Backsplash Options: **Two-piece squared**
- Sink Options: **Self-rimming, undermounted, flush**
- Sizing: **Typically 1" by 1" to 24" by 24"**
- Thickness: **¼" to ⅜"**
- Finish: **Matte, glossy, textured, natural**
- Availability: **Varies by manufacturer**
- Warranty: **Depends on installer**

Ceramic tile is made from a mixture of natural clays and has been used for centuries to cover everything from floors and walls to countertops. Because of its range of colors, textures, and finishes, it is easy to coordinate with any décor—from rustic to ultra modern. Its water and stain resistance makes it a perfect choice for the kitchen and the bathroom.

Glazed ceramic tile is the most popular tile for countertops. The glaze is a glass-like material that is baked on to give the tile a hard, protective shell. Porcelain tile is more expensive, but also tougher. It is produced by firing fine white clay at extremely high temperatures, making it impervious to water. Because it starts out white, you can tint it any color. Some porcelain is tinted on the surface only. More expensive porcelain tile has consistent color throughout, making any chip far less obvious. Unglazed tile, fired at relatively low temperatures, is porous and therefore not a good choice for a work surface installed around a water source—the longer unglazed tile stays wet, the greater the chance bacteria and mildew will build up.

Tiles come in a range of shapes as well as materials, from simple squares and rectangles to ovals, octagons, and rhomboids. The square 12-inch floor tiles make great countertops because they provide a flatter surface with fewer grout lines.

While solid-color 4-inch field tiles were once the standard for a tile countertop, tile today is making more of a design statement. Tiles are available that mimic natural stone and clay bricks, and there are metallic-glaze tiles, hand-painted tiles, and tiles with embossed designs. You can arrange two complementary colored tiles in a checkerboard pattern. You can create a mosaic pattern with several colors and sizes of tiles and even tiles of different materials. To add visual interest to a plain

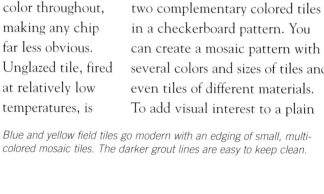

Blue and yellow field tiles go modern with an edging of small, multi-colored mosaic tiles. The darker grout lines are easy to keep clean.

countertop, consider a backsplash mural of hand-painted tiles. (But avoid using decorative wall tiles on a horizontal surface because they are softer and less water resistant than tiles made for countertops or floors.)

Despite its versatility, tile has a few disadvantages, especially when used in hard-working areas like kitchens or garages. It can crack or chip if you drop a heavy object on it. Also, because of the grout lines, you can end up with an uneven surface if you use tiles that aren't completely flat. And if you don't use an epoxy grout, grout lines will need to be sealed regularly to keep from staining or cracking.

ABOVE: Solid-color tiles can be arranged to create interesting patterns, such as in this three-color kitchen countertop.

RIGHT: A strip of small blue and white tiles adds a sophisticated detail to a green tile countertop and backsplash.

The cost of tiles varies dramatically, depending on the manufacturer, the retailer, and the quality of the tile. Mass-produced glazed tiles can cost as little as 35 cents apiece, while fancier handmade specialty tiles can range anywhere from $10 to $150 each. Consider using less expensive tiles for large expanses and a few specialty tiles for accents—across the countertop or as a backsplash. You can also save by installing the tiles yourself.

natural stone tile

- **Installed Price:** $11–$30 per square foot
- **Edging Options:** Self-edging, wood trim, metal trim, stone radius edging tiles, ceramic bullnose or V-cap
- **Backsplash Options:** Two-piece squared
- **Sink Options:** Self-rimming, undermounted
- **Sizing:** 12" by 12"
- **Thickness:** ³⁄₈"
- **Finish:** Glossy, flamed, honed, antiqued
- **Availability:** Varies by tile
- **Warranty:** None

The hottest countertop material for kitchens, bathrooms, and patios today is natural stone, but the price of a slab of stone is high. Stone tile is a great alternative that provides the rich beauty and texture of natural stone at a fraction of the cost. Most stone is available in 12-inch tiles, perfect for a 24-inch-deep countertop.

Natural stone has gained a reputation for durability as well as beauty (see pages 44–49). It is heat resistant, hard to chip, and will last forever if it is properly maintained. The best stones for countertop installations have been polished to a shiny surface to repel moisture. While all stone should be sealed to avoid staining, tiles that have been tumbled or honed for a softer texture may need sealing more often.

Most stone tiles come in 12-inch squares with straight edges.

A polished granite tile countertop with a self-edge gives the impression of a more expensive stone slab.

They are cut as precisely as ceramic tile, but since stone is a natural product, the pattern on the tiles will not be the same. When you buy stone tile, it's important to make sure all tiles come from the same color lot and that you buy enough extras to account for any breakage. Two of the same kind of stone tiles purchased weeks apart may be dramatically different in tone or pattern.

Installing stone tile is as easy as installing ceramic tile. The one difference is that grout lines are generally thinner between stone tiles to make the work surface feel more like a stone slab. A grout color that approximates the dominant color of your tile helps support that look. Also, consider using an epoxy grout, which is stronger than other types and does not need to be sealed. An epoxy grout also forms a better bond with a wooden edge.

There are several different ways you can edge natural stone tile. A wooden edge, using flat or decorative wood trim, can be affixed to the outer edge of a length of tiles. A ceramic bullnose, V-cap, or metal edge will often coordinate well with tile. Some fabricators offer natural stone radius edging tiles. One of the cleanest solutions is a self-edge. A growing number of independent stone tile cutters will bullnose or polish edges of stone. Ask your tile supplier for a reference, and allow an extra week for this work to be done before you install the tile.

Flamed slate tiles have a rustic texture that works well in bathrooms, but may be too rough for kitchen work surfaces.

Tumbled stone tiles are informal yet sophisticated, and smooth enough to use anywhere.

plastic laminate

- **Installed Price:** $15–$80 per square foot
- **Edging Options:** Seamless radius, beveled, square-edged (using laminate, solid surface, or wood band)
- **Backsplash Options:** Coved, two-piece squared
- **Sink Options:** Self-rimming
- **Sizing:** Sheets in 36", 48", 60" depths by 8', 10', 12' lengths
- **Thickness:** $\frac{1}{16}$" approximately
- **Finish:** Matte, glossy, honed, textured
- **Availability:** 1–2 weeks
- **Warranty:** 1 year on material only

Plastic laminate is made by sandwiching thin sheets of paper between two layers of clear plastic. The plastic and paper layers are combined at high pressure and temperature to create a durable surface material that is then bonded to a plywood or fiberboard substrate. The color and pattern you see in the finished product is the top layer of the decorative paper. The clear plastic protects the paper from moisture and abrasion.

The major advantages of plastic laminate are wide color choice, lower cost, stain resistance, and ease of cleanup. It is a product that can be used in almost any indoor application, from the kitchen and bathroom to the laundry room, home office, and garage. There are literally hundreds of colors and patterns to choose from, with new ones becoming available as design trends change. Plastic laminate, because of its sleek finish, is a great material to complement modern décor. While white is universal, bold colors or patterns can create a strong design statement.

If you prefer more traditional styling, you can use plastic laminate to achieve the look of natural

A plastic laminate surface transforms a simple kitchen into a '50s diner with the addition of chrome edging.

stone, wood, or even metal at a fraction of the cost of the real thing. In fact, some manufacturers offer finishes that mimic the patina or crevices of etched or honed stone. Metal look-alikes are available in raised patterns, such as diamonds and squares, as well as brushed and powdered textures. Some wood-grain laminates actually use a thin veneer of real wood under the plastic, instead of paper, combining the look of wood with the easy maintenance of plastic laminate.

While plastic laminate is a versatile product, it is not as durable as other options. Heat or sharp objects can damage it—you should never cut anything on the material—and applying harsh chemicals will cause surface blemishes. Minor damage to plastic laminate can be repaired, but most repairs will be visible. Another small disadvantage, which other synthetic materials don't have, is that its corner seams will be visible.

Not all plastic laminates are identical. The most durable laminates use a greater number of sheets of paper under the plastic layer, providing increased impact resistance and resilience. Some higher-end laminates retain color throughout the sheet, which means scratches won't be as noticeable and seams that meet at an angle won't show a brown edge. Depending on your needs, you can find laminates that are chemical resistant (good in areas where you might use harsh chemicals or cleaning agents), fire retardant, or guaranteed to be more abrasion or scuff resistant than the standard product.

TOP: Plastic laminate on a hardwood plywood substrate is suspended above its base cabinet with metal pegs.

BOTTOM: Inexpensive plastic laminate adds rich color to a white kitchen. See page 76 for instructions on how to make your own.

wood

- **Installed Price: $10–$200 per square foot**
- **Edging Options: Unlimited**
- **Backsplash Options: One piece, two-piece squared**
- **Sink Options: Self-rimming, undermounted**
- **Sizing: Custom**
- **Thickness: Varies; butcher block is typically 1½",
  2¼", and 3" thick**
- **Finish: Oiled, varnished, lacquered**
- **Availability: 1–6 weeks for butcher block;
  4–5 weeks for solid wood**
- **Warranty: 1 year on material only (none if used with
  undermounted sink) for finished butcher block**

The warmest material for a work surface is wood—for both its look and feel. Its natural finish and varied graining patterns can be sophisticated, contemporary, or rustic, depending on which wood species and stain color you use. Wood complements almost any other material and softens a room with hard surfaces such as metal or stone. Because you can cut and carve it, you can customize wood for any kind of installation.

Wood is resilient, and minor blemishes are easy to repair. Glasses or dishes dropped on wood have a good chance of survival, and most chips or scratches can be sanded out. Depending on how wood is finished, it can be used for any work surface inside or outside the home.

However, wood is not heat-proof, so if you install it near a stove, have a trivet on hand for hot pots and pans. Or you can install metal heat bars in the wood top to serve as a permanent trivet. Because wood can be scratched, stain or oil it frequently, using a nontoxic product wherever food is prepared or served. An untreated wood surface can also absorb moisture, creating a rich environment for bacteria growth, so it's important to clean it well after food preparation.

Different kinds of wood are more appropriate for different tasks. A maple butcher block is the ideal choice for the kitchen because it is hard but won't dull knife blades; you can also chop on the surface without worry, because scratches and dents only add to its well-worn character.

The most durable butcher blocks have an end-grain work surface with thick, 4-inch boards running vertically. The strongest are made with finger joints just below the surface. You can purchase a butcher block prefinished or unfinished: an unfinished block needs to be sanded, filled, trimmed to size, edged, and finished, but doing it yourself can save a lot of money. Butcher blocks can be set into another countertop material or wrapped around an existing top.

Exotic hardwoods, such as cherry, mahogany, walnut, and teak, can be purchased as solid or edge-joined surfaces. You can cut on them, but, because of their

A maple butcher-block countertop is not only beautiful, but it provides a durable work surface.

expense, you should treat them more like fine furniture. Make sure exotic wood you choose comes from sustainable forestry. Softer woods, such as pine and poplar, should be used in indoor areas where they won't be subjected to extreme abuse. Fir, redwood, and cedar are ideal for potting tables or outdoor countertops because they tend to be the most resistant to decay and insect infestation. Teak has the best water resistance. For outdoor work surfaces where you serve food or pot edible plants, avoid using

ABOVE: The reddish hues of this varnished hardwood vanity add warmth to an all-white bathroom.

RIGHT: A slab of thick butcher-block takes on a shiny patina after years of use.

pretreated wood or any toxic chemical preservatives, varnishes, or stains. You can paint lower grades of softwood and finish them with a protective varnish. For a very rustic look, you can use old planks of recycled wood.

richlite

- **Installed Price:** $50–$80
- **Edging Options:** Wide variety
- **Backsplash Options:** Two-piece squared
- **Sink Options:** Self-rimming, undermounted
- **Sizing:** Sheets up to 60" by 144"
- **Thickness:** ¾" to 1½"
- **Finish:** Matte
- **Availability:** 3–4 weeks
- **Warranty:** Lifetime

I f you like the idea of wood but prefer a low-maintenance product, Richlite® is the perfect alternative. Richlite is made from resin-treated paper that derives from either sustainable forests in North America or hemp from Ecuador and the Philippines. It is an environmentally friendly, nonporous material with a natural look and soft feel somewhat like wood. Unlike some other manufactured products, no hazardous waste is generated in the production of Richlite. While this is a new product for the home, it has been used for years for marine and industrial purposes as well as for skate-park surfaces.

Richlite countertops come in a limited number of attractive matte colors, from tan to dark blue, to complement a variety of styles. Like wood, the lighter colors will develop a natural patina with age, darkening if exposed to natural light. Unlike real wood, Richlite is heat resistant up to 350º. It also resists moisture and is relatively stain resistant. You can avoid any staining by keeping the countertops sealed. Although it is much harder than wood, Richlite can be scratched or gouged, so it is not a good surface for cutting. But since color runs throughout the material, scratches won't show a color difference. You can repair most minor scratches and nicks with a light refinishing; however, deeper gouges are not repairable.

One of Richlite's major attributes is that it is so strong it can span more than average lengths without supports; the material will not bend or break. It is a great material for an eating counter or an island top that cantilevers over its base. Generally, ¾-inch-thick material can extend beyond its base up to 12 inches. One-inch-thick material is stable up to 18 inches and 1½-inch-thick material is stable up to 24 inches. This makes Richlite a great choice for your home office or hobby room, or anywhere you want a long surface supported only by end legs.

Richlite's versatility includes moisture resistance, making it a good alternative to wood around sinks.

The dark, even color of this Richlite countertop makes a sophisticated statement in a contemporary kitchen. Since Richlite is very strong and can span longer-than-average lengths, it's an excellent and environmentally friendly choice for large surfaces.

ABOVE: Richlite can be cut to any shape, such as a triangle for the vanity top at the top, and carved to create a beveled opening for an undermounted sink (bottom).

solid surface

- Installed Price: **$50–$110**
- Edging Options: **Unlimited**
- Backsplash Options: **Coved, two-piece squared**
- Sink Options: **Integral, flush, self-rimming, undermounted**
- Sizing: **Custom**
- Thickness: **1/2"**
- Finish: **Matte, semigloss, high gloss**
- Availability: **7–10 working days**
- Warranty: **Limited 10–15 years on material and labor**

Solid-surface material, also known by its brand names such as Corian and Wilsonart, is a nonporous product that busy homeowners love for its durability, consistent color, and seamless appearance. It is stain, heat, scratch, moisture, and fade resistant, and one of the lowest-maintenance work surface options. While solid-surface material can look like stone, it is soft and warm to the touch. But unlike stone, it is almost impossible to chip or break, and it's resilient enough that a glass dropped on it won't break. Very hot items can damage the surface and nicks and scratches can result from misuse. But all damage can be repaired.

Because solid surface is a manufactured product, created by combining natural minerals with resin and various additives, it can be formed and molded to any shape you wish. Any size sink can be integrated into a countertop in a one-piece construction. Drainboards and soap trays can also be molded into the surface. You can create almost any countertop or desk edge treatment you can think of, as well as inlay a different color or material along the edge or into the surface.

From a design standpoint, solid surface is an extremely versatile material. But it doesn't come cheaply: it's almost as expensive as some natural stone and every extra detail will add to its price. In addition, because of its consistent color and texture, it looks artificial when it is compared to real stone.

The strongest solid-surface products are made with acrylic resin rather than polyester. Most of the big manufacturers now use acrylic, and each offers a large selection of unique colors. Since most manufacturers honor their warranties only if a certified contractor installs the product, it is a good idea to use a product line represented by your installer.

At the far left, an integral white sink is part of a solid-surface vanity top, while at near left the inlaid white stripes give character to a sleek solid surface desktop.

One of the benefits of solid surface is that it can be formed in any shape you want, such as this multi-angled corner treatment.

glass

- Installed Price: **$75–$150**
- Edging Options: **Square, beveled, radius**
- Backsplash Options: **Two-piece squared**
- Sink Options: **Self-rimming, undermounted, flush**
- Sizing: **Custom**
- Thickness: **¼" to ⅜"**
- Finish: **Clear, sandblasted, etched**
- Availability: **1–3 weeks**
- Warranty: **None**

A sleek clear-glass sink sits on top of a textured glass countertop, providing contrast while keeping the sophisticated look intact.

Long used for desktops and coffee tables, glass has now found its place in kitchens and bathrooms. Sleek and sophisticated, glass is also versatile. Left clear it will complement any color scheme. An etched or sandblasted design on the back of a glass sheet will obscure the view through the top and add visual texture to a room. By painting a color on the back you can match your work surface to colors in the rest of the room. Curved edges will soften an angular room.

Sheets of manufactured glass typically come in ¼-inch to 1-inch thicknesses. Handmade bubble glass and other artisan glass can be made to your specifications. Glass generally comes in rectangular sheets, but you can have it cut to any shape, including half circles and trapezoids, to meet the most contemporary design specifications. Since glass is heatproof, waterproof, and stainproof, it is a good choice for eating areas as well as bathroom vanities. Additionally, it can be used with an undermounted sink, which will require support at the cabinet level. In the most modern applications, glass is floated above a base with sleek stainless steel bolts. When used as a desktop or conventional countertop, it is often set into a wood or metal frame.

Glass is not a great choice for a busy household, especially one with active children. The surface can be scratched and greasy fingers will leave countless marks; even clean fingers will leave visible marks. While you can easily clean off both liquids and solids, watermarks will remain if you don't towel-dry the surface. If you like the sleek look and feel of glass, consider small glass tiles that can be used in a backsplash or interspersed with other tiles throughout a countertop.

Designs painted onto the underside of the glass make this countertop a work of art.

TOP: Translucent glass extends beyond a peninsula base to provide an elegant and contemporary countertop eating area.

LEFT: Because the clear-glass top has been mounted on the wall, a small bathroom feels spacious.

41

engineered stone

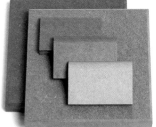

- ■ Installed Price: $60–$130
- ■ Edging Options: Square, beveled, radius
- ■ Backsplash Options: Square
- ■ Sink Options: Self-rimming, undermounted
- ■ Sizing: Custom
- ■ Thickness: $^3/_8$", $^3/_4$", $1^1/_4$"
- ■ Finish: Glossy (Quartz), matte (SlateScape)
- ■ Availability: 4 weeks
- ■ Warranty: Limited 10 years on material and labor

Engineered stone is the newest category of surfacing material. The most common product is made of up to 95% quartz crystals and referred to as Quartz. It provides the benefits of natural stone with several unique advantages. There is no need to seal, polish, or recondition Quartz to maintain its natural luster. It is resistant to stains as well as heat. And while it is a natural product, it has no grains below the surface to absorb moisture, eliminating the potential for bacterial growth and making it one of the safest natural surfaces for food preparation.

Quartz is a luxury product, as elegant as it is trouble free. Its quartz crystals absorb and reflect light, adding depth and visual texture to its rich colors, which include a wide range of neutrals as well as a deep blue and bright red. The surface material blends well with other natural products, including tile, glass, metal, and wood. It can be used in any room, but because of its price—its only real disadvantage—it is suggested for use in kitchens and bathrooms.

You can cut a sheet of Quartz to meet your exact specifications and purchase strips or tiles to use for a backsplash. You can also add an inlay of a contrasting color or material into the countertop or backsplash for a decorative effect. Quartz is so hard that it would take a cut diamond or other quartz crystals to scratch it. It is also so strong that it can span up to 36 inches or overhang up to 12 inches without support. Because it is stone, seams between sheets will show. But it is created in a raw sheet size of 52 inches by 118 inches, so you can cut a large L-shaped counter or desktop from a single sheet.

A lesser-known product is synthetic slate. SlateScape is available in four colors and six edge treatments. It is a fiber cement–based product and is stronger and more durable than most natural stone, making it unlikely to scratch. It is also resistant to high temperatures. However, it is porous and needs sealing. SlateScape can be repaired if damaged.

Engineered stone offers several bright colors that can add visual excitement to a room.

FAR LEFT: Beige or white engineered stone is a trouble-free alternative to the popular light marble and sandstone.

LEFT: An engineered stone countertop is matched with a quarter circle of butcher-block to create a handsome eating area.

BOTTOM: You can use SlateScape for every work-station in your kitchen and not worry about scratching, burning, and staining.

natural stone

- **Installed Price: $70–$200**
- **Edging Options: Various**
- **Backsplash Options: Square**
- **Sink Options: Self-rimming, undermounted**
- **Sizing: Custom**
- **Thickness: ¾", 1¼"**
- **Finish: Polished, honed, tumbled, flamed, filled**
- **Availability: 4 weeks**
- **Warranty: None**

A drainboard has been carved into the granite countertop next to the sink for a clutter-free look.

With its variegated patterns and color nuances, natural stone is the mark of luxury in today's kitchens, baths, home offices, and patio entertainment areas. Each slab of stone is unique because it is cut from the earth, not manufactured. Thus, no two pieces of stone are identical, which can add to the fun of selecting a slab for your home.

Stone is growing in popularity because it's beautiful and long lasting. While stone purchased for work surfaces was once limited to what was available at the local quarry, today you can choose stones from all over the world. Most stones come in slabs as well as 12-inch tiles (see page 30) and 4-inch lengths for backsplashes. Each kind of stone has its own characteristics. All stone offers good heat resistance. The denser the stone, the more stain and scratch resistant it will be. The advantages and disadvantages of the most popular stones for work surfaces follow.

GRANITE

Formed by volcanic activity, granite is one of the hardest and least porous rocks you can use for a countertop, which is why it is the most popular stone surface for both interior and patio kitchens. It is fairly resistant to acidic products and requires only an annual resealing. It has two kinds of color patterns: one is consistent, meaning it has the same speckled pattern throughout; and the other is variegated, with veins that swirl and vary from slab to slab. All granite consists of a percentage of crystals that shimmer when hit by light. It is generally polished, but can be honed for a softer finish or sandblasted for a rougher one.

A dark granite vanity top pairs well with warm wood in a contemporary rustic bathroom.

ABOVE: Honed granite countertops are softer in look and feel than those of highly polished stone.

LEFT: The rough edges of this granite slab match the texture of the wood siding covering the base of this countertop.

Veined marble works hand in hand with chrome fixtures to bring a neutral bathroom to life.

Marble can cool down or warm up a space, depending on its color. Here, a beige marble helps create a relaxing bathroom retreat.

MARBLE

Characterized by deep or light veins that can vary dramatically from one slab to the next, marble is softer and less dense than granite. Its color range is dramatic, from soft beiges to pinks, dark reds, oranges, and greens. Because of its color, even a small area of marble can make a large design statement.

Consider marble if you don't mind a high-maintenance material. Food acids such as lime and vinegar will stain and etch it quite easily, so the surface must be resealed frequently. However, you might like the aged quality that staining creates, and want the look for your kitchen. Serious bakers often insert a section of marble in their countertop because they consider it the ideal surface for rolling out pastry. Marbles vary in softness, so check with the supplier to make sure the one you like is suitable for your situation. Marble is available polished, honed, and tumbled.

TRAVERTINE

Less formal than marble, travertine is characterized by small pits scattered across its surface. The stone tends to be fairly soft, and the pits can soak up moisture and stains. The slab can be honed, however, and filled with grout, then sealed to preserve the surface. The warm tan hues and soft feel may make it worth the extra maintenance.

This small dressing table was cut from a solid block of silver travertine.

LIMESTONE

Like marble, limestone is soft and warm. It has a more weathered look and less graining than marble, making it more suitable for rustic or country-style homes. Limestone is generally available in beige, gray, and white, with lighter and darker veins. It's one of the most porous stones and not only stains but can pit if exposed to acids such as vinegar. French limestone is the best type to use in the kitchen; other kinds are more suitable for bathrooms. You can get the look of limestone with Jerusalem stone, which is a bit harder and less porous.

RIGHT: *The curves of the limestone countertop are repeated in the round glass sink, circular mirror, and bell-shaped sconces.*

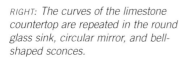

Form meets function when a round soapstone sink is set atop a soapstone counter.

SOAPSTONE

Generally a deep gray with light striations of quartz, soapstone is a soft stone with a texture that feels like a dry bar of soap. Because it's less porous than many stones, it is not affected by acidic products and will not stain below the surface. However, it can scratch or chip because of its softness. With a little elbow grease, you can scrub or sand away scratches and chips as well as surface stains. Soapstone is a good choice for kitchens because it will not harbor food bacteria. It does not have to be sealed and will develop a natural patina.

SLATE

Black, gray, or dark green in color, slate is softer than granite and marble and also less porous. Like soapstone, slate is naturally stain resistant, and while it can scratch easily, marks can be sanded out. This smooth stone traditionally has a matte finish that doesn't need sealing, but you can oil it for a shinier look. It's a good choice for outdoor applications because it is water resistant.

LAVA STONE

A French company, Pyrolave, has created a high-end countertop material that uses natural lava stone as its base. The stone is glazed with colored enamel and fired in a kiln to give it a smooth, glasslike surface. Lava stone is both dense and lightweight, with vibrant colors that can be custom matched to any décor, and is available in matte and glossy finishes. Because of its expense (about $300/square foot), this stone is best saved for luxury applications, such as a kitchen island top or master bathroom.

ABOVE: *Because of their dark gray color, slate countertops provide a quiet background for more dramatic design features in this kitchen.*

LEFT: *A bright red Pyrolave countertop takes center stage in a contemporary kitchen. A drainboard, carved into the side of the sink, illustrates the material's functionality as well as its beauty.*

concrete

- **Installed Price:** $75–$100
- **Edging Options:** Square, beveled, radius
- **Backsplash Options:** Two-piece squared
- **Sink Options:** Integral, self-rimming, undermounted
- **Sizing:** Custom
- **Thickness:** 1¾"–2"
- **Finish:** Diamond sanded, sealed, waxed
- **Availability:** 6–8 weeks
- **Warranty:** Varies

Concrete is a natural, sustainable material that is gaining popularity for its low-sheen finish and artistic appeal. It can be cast to include an integral sink and other features, such as built-in heat bars and cutting boards.

While concrete itself is nothing more than cement, lightweight aggregate, and additives, each concrete countertop is unique, with subtle variations in color and finish. Mottled colors are created by embedding glass or marble chips into the surface. Some artisans also offer veined, marble-like textures as well as clean monotones. Some surfaces are polished to a low-sheen finish while others have an exposed sand-aggregate finish. You can personalize countertops by embedding fossils, medallions, coins, or other items in the surface. Because of the labor and artistry that go into making them, concrete countertops are considered a luxury product.

Concrete takes more care than other countertop materials. Since it is porous, it can absorb moisture left on it for an extended period, and it will stain if the sealer is compromised. Acids such as lemon, wine, and vinegar can etch the surface. Knives can damage the sealer. Extreme heat won't hurt the concrete itself, but can burn and crack the sealer. Concrete will often develop hairline cracks as a result of shrinkage. However, these cracks are nonstructural and, for those who love the material, add to the handmade, natural quality of the work surface.

A concrete countertop can be precast in a workshop or cast on top of your base cabinets. Most fabricators discourage homeowners from trying to build concrete countertops themselves. The concrete in a countertop is not the same as in a concrete patio. It is much harder to formulate as well as to finish if you want a durable, smooth surface with minimal hairline cracking. Normal concrete has a strength of 3,500 psi, while precast countertops have strengths up to 15,000 psi.

Through trial and error, fabricators have developed their own proprietary concrete mixes and structural reinforcement systems, including wire mesh, fiber, fiberglass, and rebar. They also have

A concrete countertop will complement any design scheme, but is especially suited to contemporary designs.

Colorful mosaic tiles were embedded in concrete to create this one-of-a-kind vanity top.

their own methods for curing, polishing, and sealing their countertops. Few are willing to share their secrets. Even if they did, the whole process takes practice to perfect, and most homeowners don't have time for the learning curve.

Look for a fabricator with experience and good references, and find out how well his or her installed countertops have held up over time. Ask which reinforcement system is used and how far the surfaces can span without support: a concrete top should be able to span up to three feet with no special attention. Also ask which sealer is used to protect the concrete. Epoxy sealers, which are more expensive and take longer to apply, are considered superior and require less maintenance once they've been applied.

If you want to tackle the job of building your own countertop, look for one of the new concrete countertop mixes and kits now on the market. They contain the additives needed to strengthen the concrete and, in some cases, all the tools you need. Do a trial casting before creating an entire surface, and practice various finishing techniques.

Strips of metal were embedded in this concrete countertop to create a built-in trivet for hot pots and pans. While heat won't burn the concrete, it can crack the sealer.

51

metal

- Installed Price: $60–$160
- Edging Options: Square, beveled, bent, no-drip
- Backsplash Options: One-piece
- Sink Options: Integral, self-rimming
- Sizing: Custom
- Thickness: Counter edging is typically 1½"
- Finish: Polished, brushed, textured
- Availability: 3–8 weeks
- Warranty: Varies; limited against defects only

A rustproof zinc top is a great surface for flower arranging. You can make your own zinc-topped table with the instructions on page 90.

Metal, while contemporary in look, is a durable, heat-resistant, stain-proof, hygienic material that has withstood the test of time. Copper and zinc are traditional metals that often are seen in period design schemes. Stainless steel, which was not invented until 1912, is associated with modern architecture.

Today you can purchase both solid and laminate metal work surfaces to use in almost any room in your home as well as outdoors. Stainless steel and copper are the most popular metals for kitchens and bathrooms, and zinc is often used outside for patio cooking areas or potting tables. While zinc and copper will change color over time if not polished, many people prefer the rich, dark-gold patina of aged copper and the soft, blue-gray patina of aged zinc.

One of the advantages of metal is that it can be fabricated to your exact specifications. Integral sinks, drainboards, and curved, no-drip or bent edges are all possible with metal. Solid and laminate metal come with decorative textures, including raised dots and squares, microperforations, and corrugated lines and patterns. A textured surface might not be ideal for food preparation areas, but will add modern detail to dining counters, serving areas, and desks.

Metal can be cold to both the eye and the touch. Therefore, it is often paired with warmer materials such as wood or natural stone. It can scratch easily and shows both water and grease marks if not cleaned and dried properly. And while scratches in copper and zinc can add to the natural patina, in stainless steel they can look messy. A brushed or textured finish will hide both scratches and marks better than a polished one.

When you select metal for a work surface, look for material that is at least $\frac{1}{16}$ inch to $\frac{1}{20}$ inch thick. Anything thinner may dent. Metal is difficult to repair once dented or heavily scratched.

The ultimate in modern design, this integral stainless steel sink and vanity top combine to form a true piece of art.

A copper countertop is the ultimate in luxury, but demands careful maintenance to retain its beauty.

projects

D epending on the material you choose, installing a countertop or work surface can be an easy do-it-yourself job. In this chapter we include 13 step-by-step projects to provide you with ideas and instructions for working with the most common materials. Other materials are not included because their warranties are honored only if licensed fabricators make and install the countertop.

All of the projects in this book assume you are starting with a prepared base. If you have new base cabinets, make sure shims have been installed both on the floor and against the wall to make the cabinets level in both directions. If you are setting a top on table legs, build the top first and then secure the legs.

If you're remodeling, you may be able to leave the old top in place, as long as the combination of the old and the new will not result in a surface that is too high. For instance, you can tile over an old laminate countertop as long as it's in sound condition. Tile itself can be covered in cement or new tile. However, it may be easier to remove the old countertop and start over.

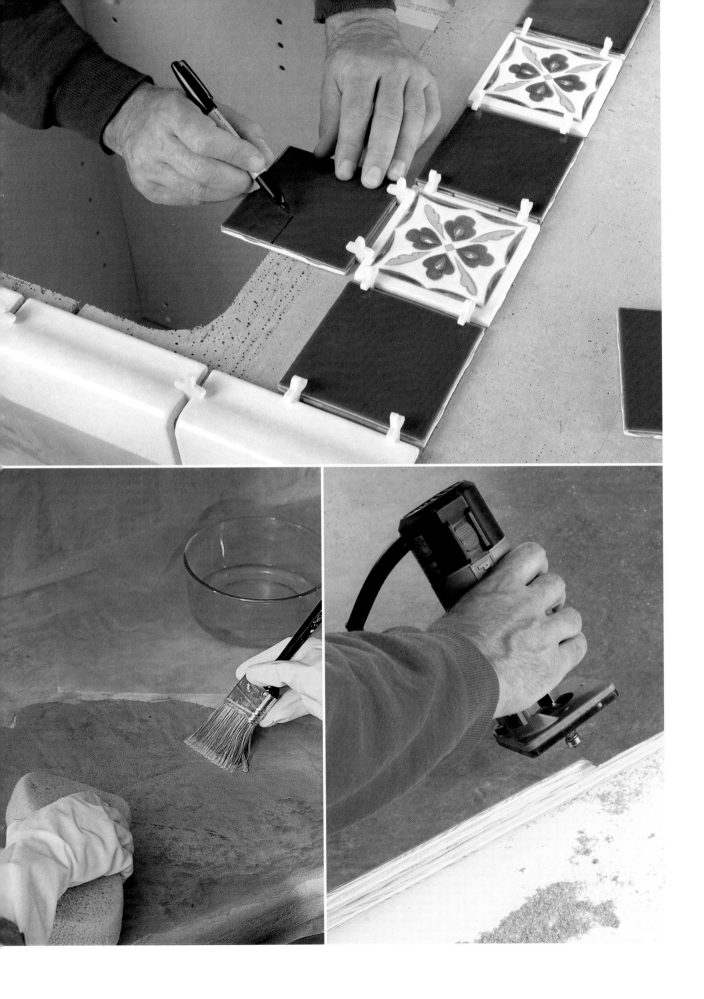

measuring

The key to a good countertop installation is taking proper measurements. Being off by even a ½ inch can result in a top that does not fit its base or leaves gaps along the back wall if the walls are not square. Typically, if you are installing a new set of cabinets, you will already have a diagram of your cabinet layout that notes the dimensions of your cabinets. If you don't have a layout or are installing a top over an old base, create your own drawing using graph paper. Your measurements should be to the nearest ⅛ inch. Also note the desired depth of any edge treatment, allowing for sufficient clearance to open drawers or doors.

REPLACING A POSTFORM COUNTERTOP

If you are replacing an existing postform top with a rounded front edge, measure the dimensions of the top as follows:

■ Measure the length of each run of countertop along the back, where the top meets the wall.

■ Measure the distance from the wall to the front of the top.

■ Measure the length of a peninsula or exposed side from the wall to the end of the piece.

■ If an exposed end is curved rather than straight, measure the distance from the wall or the edge of an appliance to the end along the midpoint of the top.

If you have diagonal inside corners, note the additional measurements, following the diagram at the bottom of the page.

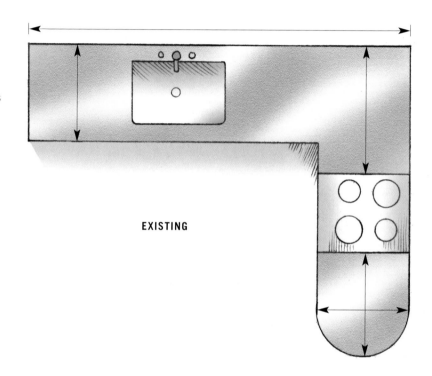

EXISTING

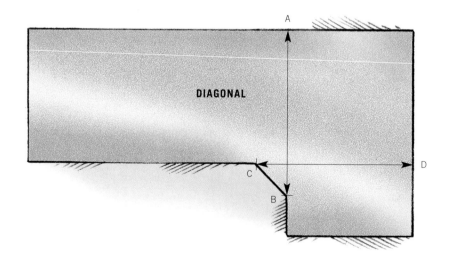

DIAGONAL

NEW CONSTRUCTION OR EXISTING STRAIGHTEDGE COUNTERTOPS

Whether you are replacing a straight-edge countertop or creating a top for new cabinets, the method of measuring is the same. If you are cutting the material yourself, add at least an inch to the final measurement for an overhang on all exposed fronts and add ½ inch to exposed sides. The overhang should meet or extend beyond the door or drawer fronts.

- Measure the length of connected cabinets along the back wall.
- Measure the depth of each cabinet segment from the outer edge of the back to the edge of the front. Do not include the thickness of a drawer or door.
- For islands, measure both the length and width of the segment of base cabinets.

TESTING FOR 90-DEGREE CORNERS

The easiest way to test a wall to make sure it is perfectly square is to take three measurements in the corner. First, measure a point along one wall 3 feet out from the corner. Next, measure a point on the adjacent wall 4 feet from the corner. Finally, measure the distance between the two points you marked. If the corner is perfectly square (a 90-degree angle), the distance between the points will be exactly 5 feet. If the distance is greater or less than 5 feet, the corner is not square.

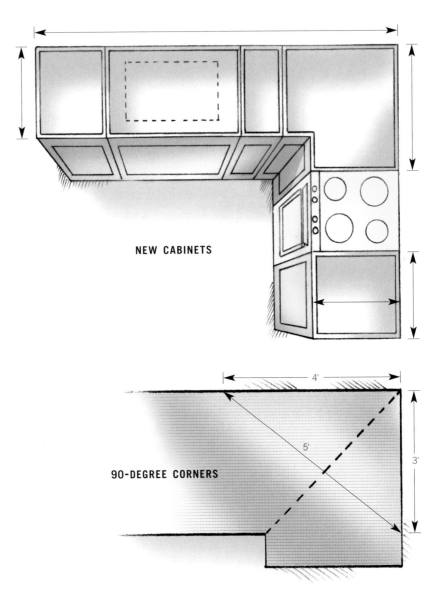

NEW CABINETS

90-DEGREE CORNERS

If there is less than a ¼-inch difference, a backsplash will cover the gap. If the difference is more, note this on your diagram. In order to duplicate the corner angle, create a paper template of the corner, which you can use when cutting your material.

CUTOUTS FOR SINKS AND APPLIANCES

Your diagram should indicate the location of walls as well as where appliances or sinks will go along a run of cabinets. If you are replacing a top, measure existing sink or drop-in stove cutouts front to back and side to side. Also note the distances from all edges to the cutouts.

MEASURE TWICE

Once you have marked all measurements on your diagram, go back and remeasure to make sure you made no mistakes. This is time consuming, but it will save you from making costly errors.

tile basics

- Plastic sheeting or construction paper
- Drop cloth
- ¾-inch plywood sheets
- ½-inch cement backerboard
- Latex-reinforced thinset adhesive
- ¼-inch notched trowel
- Screwdriver
- Carbide-tipped backerboard cutter
- 1⅝-inch deck screws
- 1¼-inch backerboard screws
- Fiberglass mesh tape

Regardless of the kind of tile you use to surface a countertop—ceramic, porcelain, or stone—the prep work and installation procedures will be the same. On the following pages we explain how to build a substrate; lay ceramic, granite, and tumbled-stone mosaic tile; edge the work surface; install a backsplash; and work around outlets or other obstructions.

Before you begin, make sure you have all the parts you need. If you are using ceramic tile, you can buy V-caps and special outside corner pieces for your front edges. For a more decorative edge treatment, purchase bullnose tiles for the front row and decorative edge tiles to run below that. Bullnose tiles can also be used to border a stove or serve as a backsplash. When you use decorative tiles for a backsplash, you may want to finish them with a quarter-round tile along the top.

Ceramic tile dealers should carry all these pieces, although they may need to special-order some of them. If you want to use granite tiles on both the surface and edges of your countertop, you'll need to bullnose the front edges of the tiles yourself or take them to a stone cutter who will do this for you. Allow time to get all materials before proceeding.

PREPARING THE SUBSTRATE

Unless you have a countertop you can tile over—such as a laminate top in decent condition—you will need to build a new substrate. Countertop tiles should rest on a surface that is solid and able to withstand moisture. The front edge must be thick enough to accommodate the edging you have chosen and the substrate needs to be level in both directions.

Professional tile setters will often install a mortar bed, because it provides a perfectly flat and smooth subsurface for the tiles. For the do-it-yourself homeowner, a layer of ¾-inch plywood topped with ½-inch or ⅓-inch cement backerboard is easier to build and will do the job well. Before you begin work, cover the front of your base cabinets with plastic sheeting or construction paper. Throw a drop cloth on the floor.

Note that if you are installing a flush-mount sink, it will be attached to the plywood before the backerboard is in place. An undermount sink will be installed after the backerboard but before tiling is installed.

1 Purchase sheets of plywood that are not warped and stack them flat until ready for use. Cut the pieces so they overhang the cabinets by about an inch. To ensure that the front and side edges are straight and square, install with the factory edges (rather than the cut edges) facing out. Attach the plywood by driving 1⅝-inch deck screws (which resist rusting) through the plywood into the cabinet base every 6 inches, making sure to countersink them. Check the entire surface to make sure it is level. If necessary, remove screws, install shims, and redrive the screws.

2 Cut a hole for the sink following the manufacturer's instructions. Most sinks come with a template you can trace onto plywood. Lower the sink into the hole to make sure it fits before proceeding. If you're installing a flush-mount sink, do so now.

Cut the backerboard pieces to fit. First, score the board several times along the cut line with a carbide-tipped backerboard knife. Then, snap the board along the scored line. You may need to cut through the fiberglass facing on the back side of the backerboard to separate the pieces. Size and arrange the pieces so that any seams in the backerboard are offset at least 3 inches from any seams in the plywood. Lay out the pieces in a dry run and make sure the edges line up precisely with the plywood below, including the hole for the sink or any other appliances. Test to make sure that the sink will fit. For a flush-mount sink, bring the backerboard up to the sink edge.

3 Mix a batch of latex-reinforced or epoxy thinset adhesive. Spread thinset over the plywood using a ¼-inch notched trowel, spreading just enough for one backerboard piece each time. Install one piece of backerboard at a time. Lay the backerboard in the thinset and drive 1¼-inch backerboard screws in a grid, spaced about 6 inches apart.

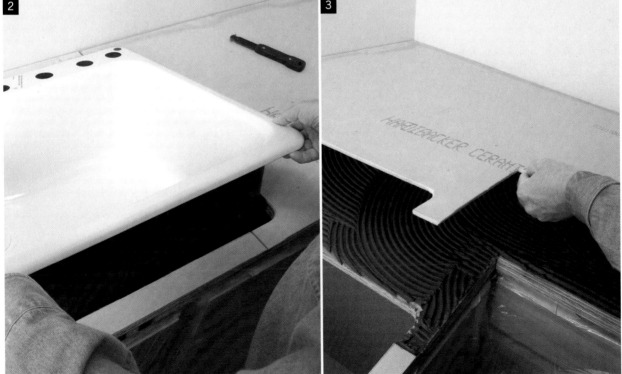

4 If the backsplash will be tiled with radius bullnose or quarter-round trim at the top, cut pieces of backerboard to accommodate the thickness and width of the backsplash. Spread the back of the strips with thinset and press them into place against the wall. Bullnosed field tiles or decorative border tiles can be set directly against the wall.

5 Apply fiberglass mesh tape to the backerboard joints. Also wrap the front edges of the backerboard and plywood with the tape to cover the joint between the two layers of material. Do not apply tape where the backsplash meets the countertop. Install an undermount sink before tiling.

CUTTING TILE

Because of their density, most countertop tiles should be cut with a wet saw. You can rent a tile-cutting saw from a tile supplier or equipment rental store. There is a learning curve to cutting tile without breaking it, so take the time to get it right. Ask your tile supplier for chipped or broken tiles on which you can practice making cuts.

- Waterproof drop cloth (for cutting tile indoors)
- Diamond-blade wet saw
- Heavyweight gloves
- Eye goggles
- Ear protection
- Steel tape measure

1 Gather the tools you will need and set the saw on an even surface, preferably outdoors. If you are working indoors, be sure to protect the floor with a water-proof drop cloth.

2 Set the wet saw's fence (the piece that guides the tile during cutting) to the desired tile width, as indicated on the measurement bar. Use the steel tape to check the accuracy of the bar by holding one end of the tape against the fence and the other at the desired tile width. If the measurement on the bar is not exactly correct, you'll need to adjust the fence.

3 With the finished side of the tile up, cut the tile. (Cutting on this side minimizes chipping.) Don't force the tile; if sparks fly, you are pushing too hard. Use a gentle touch, allowing the blade to grind through the tile.

When working with granite or marble tile that has a visual pattern, give each tile a specific position in your countertop layout. Mark each tile with a tape label indicating that position and direction. Before cutting, remove the tape label from your tiles. When you're finished cutting, replace the tape, with the arrow going in the correct direction. If you chip a stone tile, use a fragment from the other cut tiles or use tile nippers to break off a piece to fit the chipped area. Set the tile as planned, then use silicone sealant to put the fragment in place.

4 You can make angled cuts for mitered corners by tilting the blade on the wet saw. If a tile must be cut at an angle as well as to length, make the angled cut first, test it in place for size, and then make the length cut. When making an angled cut, hold the tile against the fence as you would for any other cut. To cut two ceramic edge pieces for an inside corner, visualize how the cut should look and roughly draw the direction of the cut on the tile. Position the tile on the tray of the cutter so the tile is oriented the same way as it will be installed. Cut

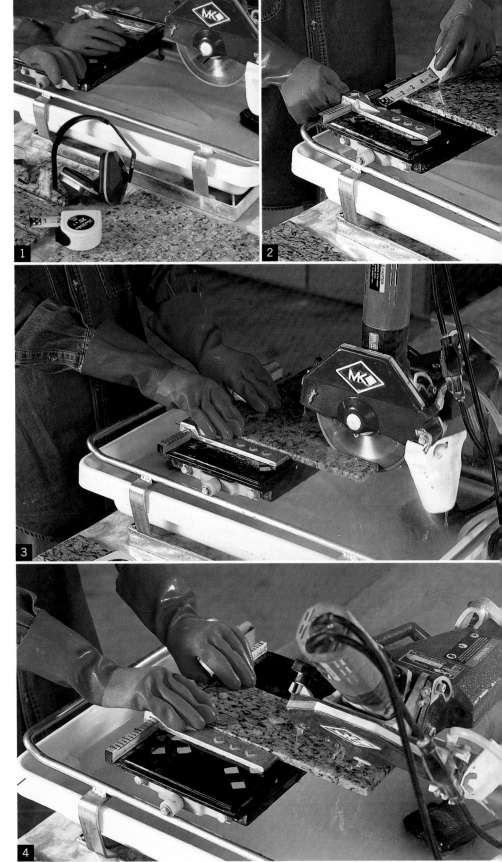

both pieces longer than they need to be so you can try again if necessary and not waste the tile.

Test the pieces for fit, using spacers, and then cut the tile to length.

PLANNING THE LAYOUT

Before you start setting tile, you need to establish a layout. Ideally, you want to use full tiles to create a symmetrical look.

1 If you are edging with V-cap tiles, set one in place and mark a line along the tile on the backerboard to indicate where the first row of field tiles will be set. Because of the thickness of the thinset, the V-caps will actually be installed ⅛ inch or so in front of this line; this allows for a grout line between the field tiles and the V-caps.

If you want a wider grout line, adjust this line inward. Make marks using the V-cap in several places and, using a straightedge, draw a continuous line across the front of the countertop. If the top has a 90-degree angle (an L-shape), continue the line straight to the wall. After you draw the guideline on the connecting piece, you will have two intersecting lines at the front edge of the inside corner.

2 Place the tiles on the substrate where you want them to go, using plastic spacers for the grout lines. (Some tiles come with self-spacing lugs or are mounted on plastic grids, so you won't need to use the spacers.) For an L-shaped countertop, start the layout at the front edge of the inside corner. The tiles will run out in both directions from there.

3 If you're working with a single rectangle, there are several ways you can start your layout. One is to mark a line through the center of the sink (in front and behind the cutout) and lay out your tiles from there. This should give you the same size tiles on either side of the sink opening. (You can also center the first tile on this line.) If you have no sink, you can start by measuring and marking the center of the top, drawing a straight line perpendicular to the front edge. Center one row of tiles along this line, front to back. Lay another along the front edge of the countertop. If the layout is not pleasing or results in partial tiles at the edges, adjust as needed. A cut tile should not be less than half the width of a full tile.

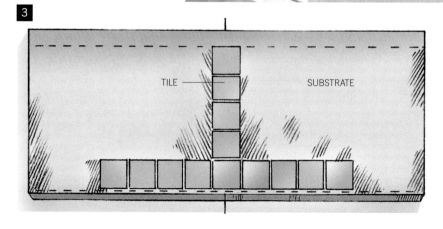

4 If your trial layout ends up with a narrow sliver at the side ends or back, slightly widening the grout lines may allow you to use only full tiles. Another solution is to adjust the layout to have two rows of smaller tiles symmetrically placed within the layout. If you have half-width tiles at only one end of a side-to-side run, you might want to redo the layout so those cut tiles run down the center of the countertop or against the sink-edge side wall.

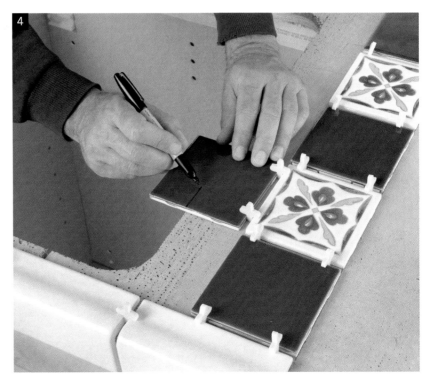

MAKING SPECIAL CUTS

Tiling a countertop may call for several complicated cuts. Before you make any cuts, take into account the thickness of the mortar. Field tiles will be about $1/8$ inch higher than they were in the dry run; edging and backsplash tiles will come forward about $1/8$ inch. These can take a few attempts before you get them right, so have extra tiles on hand. If a tile must be cut at an angle as well as to length, measure and mark the guideline, make the angled cut first, hold the tile in place, and then make your length cut.

To cut two trim pieces for an inside corner, visualize how the cut should look and roughly draw the direction of the cut on the tile. Position the tile on the tray of the cutter, orienting the tile just as it will be installed. Cut both pieces longer than they need to be, so that you can try again if it's necessary and not waste the tile. Test the pieces for fit, using spacers, and cut to length.

Make sure you understand how the pieces will all go together.

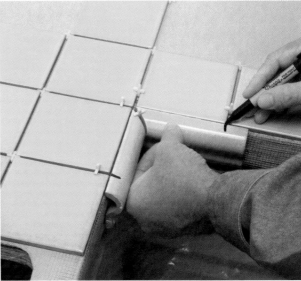

ceramic tile countertop

- **Materials for cutting (see page 60)**
- **Ceramic field tiles**
- **Tiles for edges, corners, and backsplash**
- **Latex-reinforced or epoxy thinset adhesive**
- **Latex-reinforced or epoxy grout and caulk**
- **Grout sealer**
- **¼-inch square-notched trowel**
- **Plastic spacers**
- **Tile nippers**
- **Masking tape**
- **Laminated grout float**
- **Lightweight gloves**
- **Squeegee**
- **Sponge**
- **Dry cloth**
- **Foam brush**
- **Utility knife**

Leave the dry run in place. To be sure that you can follow the layout, remove only a few linear feet of tiles at a time, set them in thinset, and then do the same for the next few linear feet of tiles. In most cases, you should set your V-cap edge tiles first. If you will be setting your field tiles right up to the front edge of the countertop, set the field tiles first and then attach the edge band.

1 Following the manufacturer's directions, mix as much latex-reinforced or epoxy thinset adhesive as you can use in half

an hour. If the thinset starts to harden while you are working, throw it out and mix a new batch. Starting at the center point of the sink or your center reference line and working along the front edge, spread the thinset onto the backerboard using a ¼-inch square-notched trowel. To ensure a flat surface for the tiles, hold the trowel at the same angle the entire time and scrape away any globs of thinset.

2 Press the tiles into the thinset. If you are using plastic spacers, position them between the tiles to keep all the grout lines the same width. Use a straightedge to make sure the lines are straight, then set a 2-by-4 block of wood diagonally across two or more tiles and tap the block with a rubber mallet. Set all the full tiles first (unless you are running a row of cut tiles down the center or along the front of the countertop). When the full tiles are in place, cut, test for size, and lay the cut tiles. If you are setting tiles around a round or an oval self-rimming sink, mark the curves on the tiles and cut them with tile nippers. The cuts don't have to be perfect because the sink rim will cover the edges.

3 When all the field tiles are laid, "butter" (spread thinset like you'd butter a piece of toast) the back of your backsplash tiles or

use a trowel to comb thinset onto the backerboard strip or the wall. Use spacers to hold the bottom backsplash piece above the field tiles the width of the grout line. If you will be adding a small quarter-round piece at the top (as shown), fill in the space above the backerboard strip with plenty of thinset so the quarter-round can nest in it. Butter the back of the quarter-round and press it in place. If necessary, use strips of masking tape to hold the pieces together while they set.

4 Either butter the edging tiles with thinset or apply thinset to the vertical edge of the countertop. If the edging attaches primarily to the vertical substrate edge, use masking tape to hold the tiles in place until the thinset sets. Use spacers to position the edging pieces and hold them firmly in place while you apply the tape. Every few minutes, check that the edging pieces haven't slipped down. If so, you may need to reposition them and reapply the tape.

5 Allow the thinset to harden overnight. Remove the spacers. Mix the grout and then spread it diagonally across the tiles with a laminated grout float, forcing the grout into the gaps between the tiles. Squeegee away the excess, working diagonally across the joints to avoid digging out grout.

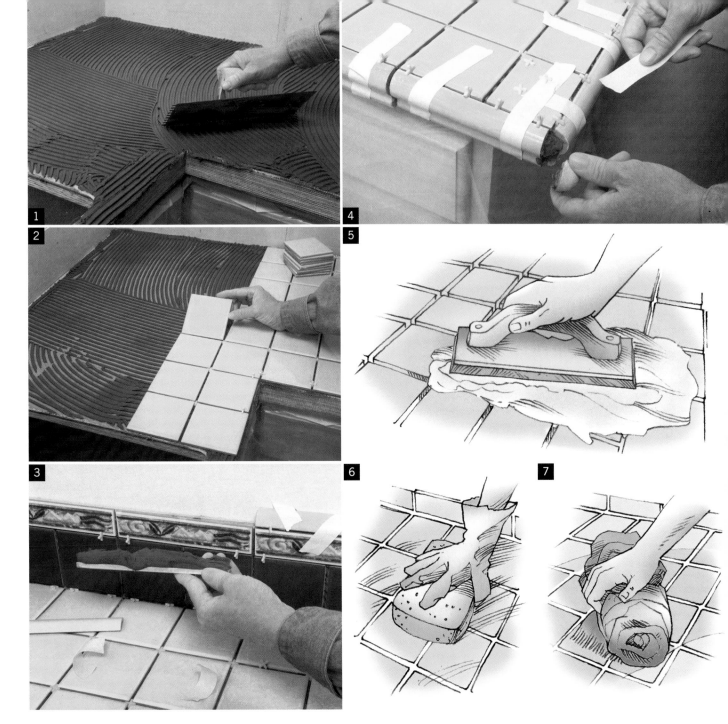

6 When finished grouting, wipe the tile surface in a circular motion with a clean, damp sponge. Be sure to wear gloves because grout is alkaline and will irritate your skin. Continue until all grout is cleaned off the tiles, rinsing and wringing out the sponge often; be careful not to dig into the grout lines. Then run the sponge parallel to the grout lines to smooth the lines down a little below the level of the tile.

7 Allow the grout to dry, then buff with a dry, lint-free cloth. If holes appear, fill with grout.

Unless you use an epoxy grout, the grout should be sealed to make it more water and mildew resistant. Wait until the grout is thoroughly set (at least 24 hours and up to a few weeks). Then, apply the sealer to the grout lines with a foam brush. Wipe off any sealer from glazed tiles before it dries.

To ensure a waterproof joint at the back of the countertop, use a utility knife to cut away the grout along the bottom of the back-splash. Apply a bead of caulk to this joint.

granite tile countertop

- Materials for cutting (see pages 60–61)
- Granite tiles
- Latex-reinforced or epoxy thinset adhesive
- ¼-inch notched trowel
- Graph paper
- Blue painter's tape
- Plastic cross spacers
- Wood corner molding
- Latex-reinforced or epoxy grout and caulk
- Laminated grout float
- Lightweight gloves
- Sponge and bucket of water
- Dry cloth
- Granite and grout sealer
- Acrylic polyurethane finish
- Carpenter's level
- Finishing nails

Granite tile is less expensive and easier to install than a solid slab of stone. When you establish narrow grout lines, the finished effect looks like slab, with all its advantages. Because the tiles are 12-inch squares, you can lay a 25-inch-wide countertop without having to cut any tiles, providing you use a ⅛-inch grout line and a wood corner molding that covers the front ¾ inch of the top. When creating your layout, try to use uncut tiles in each corner, then adjust the size of the remaining tiles to fit.

This project uses full 12-inch tiles to create a backsplash. You can also cut the tiles in half to create a 6-inch-high backsplash. The top edges of all the backsplash

tiles should be bullnosed for a finished look unless they meet the bottom of a cabinet. If the backsplash does not end at a wall, the exposed sides of each end tile should also be bullnosed.

1 Hold the wood molding against the corresponding edges and draw a pencil line along each

length, marking the backerboard. This line will be your outer grout line. Then, at the desired grout width (⅛ inch for this project), carefully draw the inner grout line. Working with this line as your guide, draw your countertop to scale on a piece of graph paper.

Sketch the tile layout, allowing for the grout lines between the

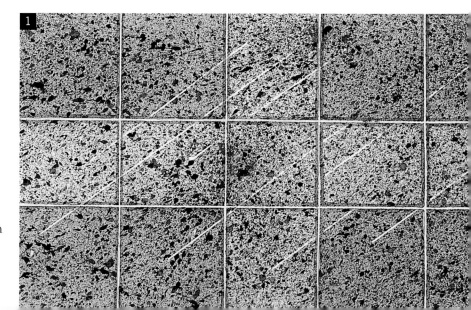

tiles and around the edges. Number the drawn tiles and include directional arrows for grain line or pattern if the tile has either.

2 Before you set the tile, do a dry-run layout on the counter, using tile spacers at each corner to ensure that the tiles meet at right angles. Make sure you like the way each tile looks next to those around it. Adjust if necessary. Label each tile with a piece of blue painter's tape marked with the tile number and orientation, matching the numbers on your tiles to those in your drawing. Note on the label if a tile needs to be cut. Cut the tiles as necessary and position them in the layout to make sure they fit. If necessary, recut. When the fit is perfect, remove the tiles.

3 Apply the thinset to the backerboard with the ¼-inch notched trowel, stopping at the inner grout lines you marked in Step 1. Place a corner tile along the inner grout lines. Set the tile straight down, parallel to the surface. Place spacers at each corner.

4 Place the next tile, aligning it with the first tile and fitting it snugly against the spacers. Check the surface with a carpenter's level and adjust the tiles if necessary. Continue laying the tiles in your prearranged pattern, adding spacers between tiles. Keep checking your work with a level. Allow the thinset to dry for 24 hours.

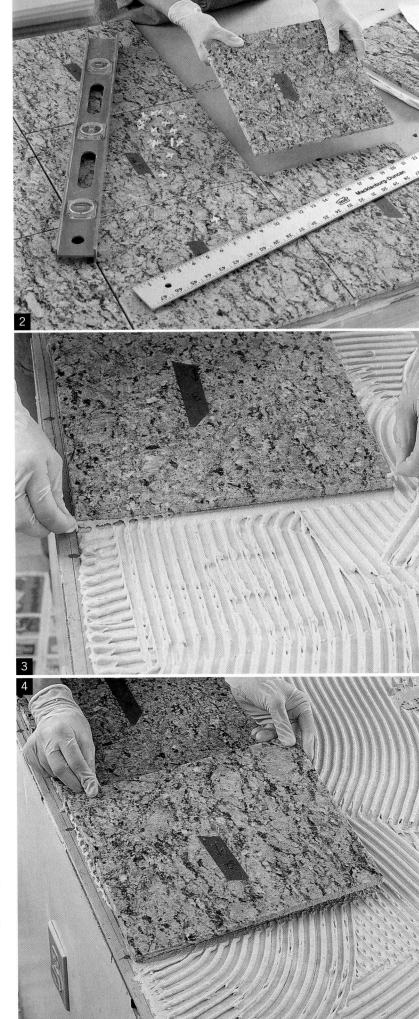

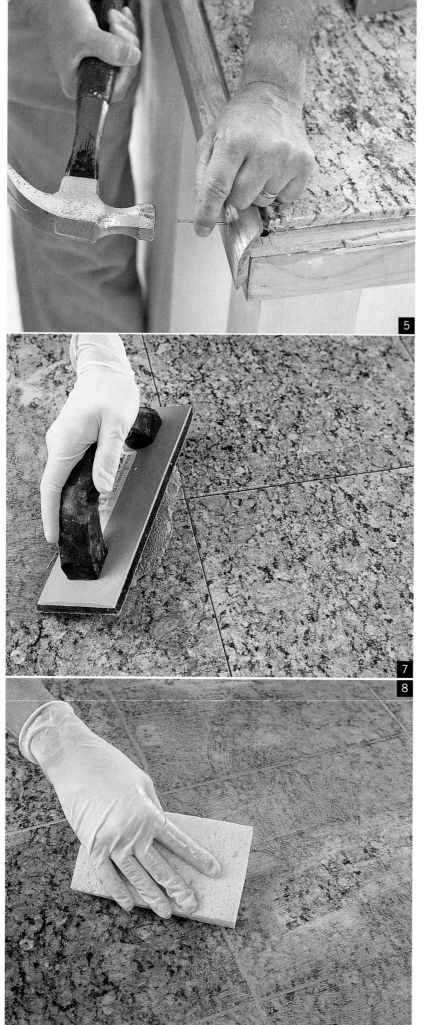

5 Finish the trim, sanding it and then sealing it with several coats of acrylic polyurethane finish to protect it from moisture. Attach the trim, securing it with finishing nails through the plywood substrate. Tape off the trim with blue painter's tape to protect it before you apply the grout.

6 Apply thinset to the back wall, 12 inches up from the countertop, using the trowel. Use spacers to hold the bottom backsplash pieces the width of a grout line above the countertop tiles. Press the tiles against the wall and hold in place until the adhesive sets.

7 Put on gloves to protect your skin. Mix the grout according to the manufacturer's instructions. Use either epoxy grout or sanded caulk instead of regular grout on those edges where tile meets wood trim. Also use caulk between the back tiles and backsplash to prevent cracking. Holding the float at a slight angle, as shown, push the grout between the tiles, working in all directions and packing the grout as firmly as possible.

8 As soon as a haze starts to form, sponge the tile with a wrung-out, nearly dry sponge. Keep a bucket of fresh water handy to rinse the sponge often. After letting the grout cure for 24 hours, carefully seal the tile and the grout according to the manufacturer's instructions.

tiling around an outlet

If there's an outlet or a switch on the wall above the countertop, you may have to cut tiles to run around it before you can install your backsplash. If the new tile recesses an electrical box more than ¼ inch from the wall surface, install a box extender. You may also need to purchase extra-long screws to re-attach the outlet or switch.

Turn off power to the outlet. Remove the outlet cover or switch plate. You may find it easier to work if you remove the entire switch or receptacle. Carefully measure around the opening to determine the correct dimensions of the tile pieces you need to cut.

If you are using ceramic tiles, you may need to cut a corner out of one or two with tile nippers. The cut doesn't have to be perfect because as the switch plate will cover the edges. Cut the tiles as necessary and install.

When you are making a backsplash with 12-inch stone tiles, the pieces plus the opening should add up to the dimensions of one tile. Cut the tile pieces. Working on a slick surface, such as a sheet of plastic, apply silicone sealant to the cut edges of the tile pieces. The silicone will hold the pieces together long enough for you to put them up as one unit; the thinset will secure them. Treat the unit as one tile and apply it to the wall.

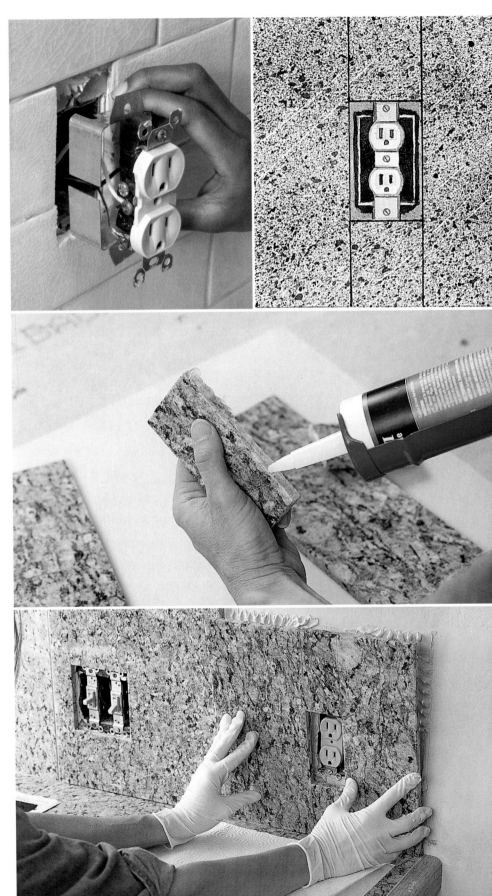

tumbled stone vanity

- Kraft paper
- Blue painter's tape
- Trisodium phosphate (TSP)
- Heavyweight rubber or latex gloves
- Eye and ear protection
- 60-grit sandpaper
- Steel tape measure
- Square-notched and notched margin trowel
- Materials for cutting (see pages 60–61)
- 4-inch stone tile
- 4-by-12-inch mosaic stone trim
- Wedge spacers
- Thinset adhesive
- Metal straightedge
- Carpenter's squares, large and small
- Tile nippers
- Carpenter's level
- Honing stone
- Masking paper
- Sponge and bucket of water
- Sanded grout
- Grout float
- Stone and grout sealer
- Silicone sealant

I t is possible to tile over an existing tile vanity top, as we show in this project. Setting tumbled stone is fairly easy to do yourself because the natural variations in the stone disguise less-than-perfect workmanship. Natural stone has an "A" side and a "B" side. Before beginning, examine your tile to determine which side you want facing out.

Unlike ceramic and granite tile, tumbled stone tiles call for wedge spacers rather than the standard cross spacers. Wedge spacers stand up between tiles, with the narrow edge toward the substrate and the wide edge out. The grout line will appear wider than the thin edge of the wedge because tumbled stone tiles are rounded.

Since "nipping" tiles around the sink openings leaves uneven edges, this project is suitable only for a vanity with self-rimming sinks. We have used the same stone tile to edge the vanity that we used for the surface. You can also use attractive tumbled stone radius edging tiles to achieve a softer effect.

Before beginning, remove sinks and fixtures. If any damage occurs during removal, such as pieces of the base tile coming loose, mix a small batch of thinset and, using the straight edge of the square-notched trowel, fill the voids to the level of the existing tile. Allow to dry overnight. Meanwhile, tape kraft paper to the front of the cabinets with blue painter's tape below the area you plan to tile. Wearing gloves to protect your hands, wash the existing surface with trisodium phosphate (TSP) to remove any oils. Allow the area to dry. Mix a small batch of thinset and comb on a little using the square-notched trowel. Dry the thinset overnight. If the thinset adheres to the surface, you can proceed after chipping the test thinset off with the straight edge of the trowel. If thinset comes off easily, you will need to rough up the surface with 60-grit sandpaper and try again.

1 Using the steel tape and a marker, measure and mark the midpoint along the front edge of the vanity. Do a dry-run layout of stone tiles along the front edge and along the midpoint, front to back, adding wedge spacers between tiles. Determine whether to center a tile on the midpoint or set tiles on either side of the midpoint. The goal is to avoid narrow cut tiles on either end of the vanity. When you have your layout, note it on a piece of paper and remove the tiles.

The first row of counter tile must overhang the front edge a distance equal to the thickness of the tile. To mark a horizontal reference line for this row, hold a tile vertically against the face of the cabinet even with the upper edge of the counter. Lay another tile on the counter so its front edge is flush with the surface of the face tile. Make a mark on the counter at the back edge of the counter tile. Measure the distance from the mark to the front edge of the vanity. Using this measurement and the metal straightedge, draw a horizontal line on the counter parallel to the front edge. Using the carpenter's square, draw a vertical reference line from the midpoint marked in Step 1 to the back.

2 Using the reference lines, lay out as many full tiles as possible on the counter, adding wedge spacers (thin edge down) between tiles. Where a tile extends into a sink opening, mark the curve on the top of the tile.

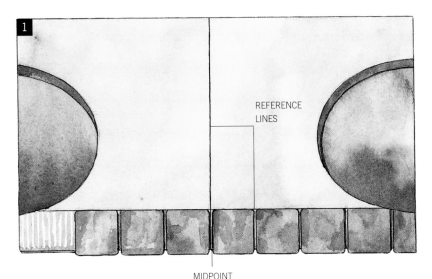

3 Put on the eye and ear protection and the gloves. On the wet saw, cut the tiles that go around the sink openings, making straight cuts $\frac{1}{8}$ inch apart toward the curve marked on each tile, as shown.

4 Using the tile nippers, break off the slivers of stone. Nip away at the remaining stone all the way to the marked curve. Don't be too concerned about perfect curves; the sink rims will cover the cuts.

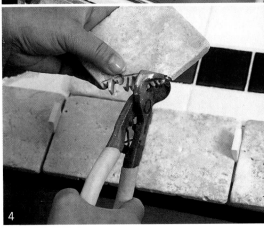

REFERENCE LINES

MIDPOINT

5 Remove the tiles in preparation for spreading the thinset adhesive. Mix the thinset according to the manufacturer's directions. Holding the straight edge of the trowel at a 30-degree angle, spread thinset on the counter in front of the horizontal reference line. Using the narrow notched edge of the trowel, comb the thinset toward the front edge.

6 Set the first row of tile as planned, starting at the midpoint and working toward the ends. Align the back edges of the tiles with the horizontal reference line and place spacers between tiles. Use the carpenter's level to check the surface; if it's not level, pry up the offending tiles, scrape off or add a little thinset, and reset. Measure, mark, and cut the last piece at each end. Then set each cut piece. Set the remaining rows from front to back using spacers between tiles and rows; cut pieces to fit against the wall at the sides and back.

7 Determine the ideal height for the face tiles based on the design of the cabinet front. Measure, mark, and cut these tiles on the wet saw. Smooth the cut edges with the honing stone, rounding them to match the tumbled edges. Using the 60-grit sandpaper, roughen the area on the cabinet front where the face tile will be set. Spread and comb on the thinset horizontally using the notched trowel. Set the face

tile under the counter tile with the cut edges down. Insert spacers between the counter and face tiles as shown; use blue painter's tape to keep the pieces from slipping. Cut the end pieces to fit; set. Use a level to make sure the face tiles are straight up and down, not tilted in or out; adjust as needed while the thinset is still wet.

8 Mosaic trim comes mounted on a back mesh. Since it's next to impossible to cut away the mesh once the piece is in place, cut away the mesh $\frac{1}{16}$ inch from the edges before setting the tile. Start the mosaic trim at the most conspicuous end of the vanity. Because the trim pieces fit into each other, cut off the projecting portion on the first piece as follows. First, rest a trim piece on the counter tile against the wall, aligning the lower edge of the trim with the edge of the counter tile. Then, insert a spacer under the trim piece near each end. Tape the upper edge of the trim piece to the wall to secure. Using the small carpenter's square, mark a cutting line as shown in photo 8.

9 Lightly mark a line on the wall at the upper edge of the trim piece with a pencil. Run this horizontal line around the vanity, making sure it is level. Before beginning to set the tile, lay kraft paper on the counter to protect the set tile. Adhere masking paper to the wall above the line you just marked to protect the

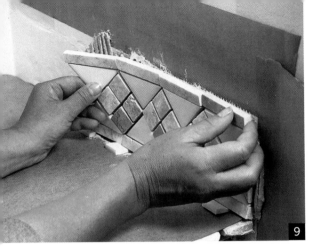

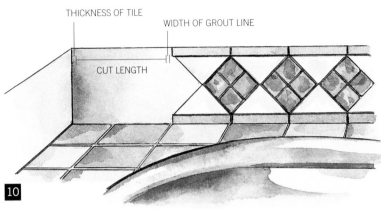

THICKNESS OF TILE

WIDTH OF GROUT LINE

CUT LENGTH

9 | 10

wall. Now, comb thinset vertically onto the wall and set the first trim piece in place, with spacers underneath. Check the upper edge with the carpenter's level. Insert spacers underneath the lower solid triangles (in this case, white) to help keep the trim from sagging.

10 To make the backsplash design flow smoothly around a corner, measure from the end of the just-set trim piece to the corner. Subtract the width of the grout line and the thickness of a trim piece to arrive at the cut length of the next trim piece (assuming the distance to the wall is less than the length of the trim piece). Measure and mark the trim piece for cutting; double-check your measurement to avoid making a cutting error. Cut the piece on the wet saw; put the leftover piece aside.

11 Comb thinset onto the wall and set the cut piece with spacers underneath; check it with the level and adjust if necessary. Set the leftover piece on the adjoining wall, positioning it away from the corner the same distance as the

previous piece. Once the surface and the upper edge are grouted, the design will appear to flow around the corner. Finish setting the backsplash around the vanity, cutting the final piece as needed. Remove the kraft paper from the countertop.

12 If you are either setting or resetting a mirror just above the backsplash, do so now. Apply the painter's tape to the J-channel on the mirror or, if there is no mirror, to the wall just above the trim. Mix the grout according to the manufacturer's instructions. Wear gloves for protection.

Holding the float at a slight angle, push the grout between the tiles, working in all directions and packing the grout as firmly as possible. Use a gloved fingertip to work grout into and between the trim pieces. If there is a mirror just above the trim, also apply grout between the lower edge of the J-channel and the trim.

13 As soon as a haze starts to form, sponge the tile with a wrung-out, nearly dry sponge. Keep a bucket of fresh water handy to rinse the sponge often.

11

14 After letting the grout cure for at least 48 hours, carefully seal the tile and the grout according to the manufacturer's instructions, using the recommended cloth. Remove the masking paper and tape from the wall.

sink options

If you are going to the trouble of putting in a new countertop, it may make sense to invest in a new sink. In selecting a sink, make sure the base cabinet opening is large enough and that there are no drawers to obstruct the plumbing. Plan to install the sink near the center of the cabinet base so it will not bump into the side of the cabinet.

Depending on the kind of sink you purchase, the installation method will vary, so choose your sink and read the installation instructions carefully before installing the plywood and backerboard substrate.

Stainless-steel sinks come in a variety of price ranges; the more expensive models have a shinier surface that is easier to clean than that of less expensive models. If you buy a stainless-steel sink, make sure that yours has sound-deadening insulation. Enameled-steel and acrylic sinks are inexpensive but not durable; spend a little more for an enameled cast-iron sink, which will stay attractive for decades.

A "self-rimming" sink is the easiest to install. Cut the sink opening in the substrate and test to see that the hole is the correct size, then tile the countertop and place the sink in the hole following the manufacturer's instructions. Save time and hassles by installing the faucets and knobs into the sink before setting the sink in place.

To put in a stainless-steel sink, apply plumber's putty to the underside of the sink and clamp the sink to the countertop using the clips provided by the manufacturer. To put in a cast-iron sink, place a bead of silicone caulk all around the hole, set the sink in the hole, and wipe away the excess caulk.

Although self-rimming sinks are simple to install, crumbs tend to collect along and under the rim. For an alternative, install a "flush-mounted" sink. First set down the plywood. Cut the hole in the plywood, install the sink, then cut and install the backerboard so it is flush with the sink. Bullnose tiles can then be installed on top of the backerboard so that they overlap the rim of the sink.

Or choose an "underhung" sink. This is the most difficult installation because of the number of cut tiles, but the result is attractive and easy to clean. Screw the sink to the underside of the plywood. Install narrow tile pieces along the vertical surface above the sink and top off the edge where it meets the countertop with bullnose tiles.

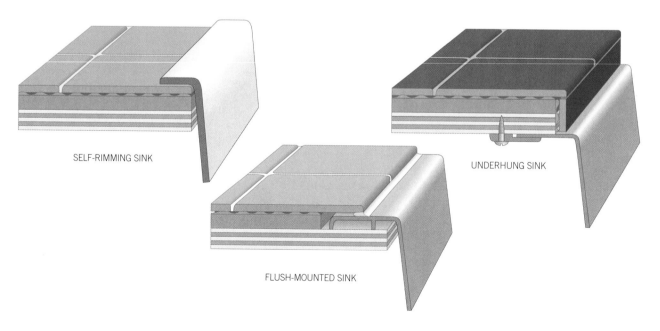

SELF-RIMMING SINK

FLUSH-MOUNTED SINK

UNDERHUNG SINK

installing a decorative backsplash

While backsplashes are generally made with the same tile used to cover the countertop, you can make a bold design statement with a decorative backsplash that covers an entire wall. This is especially common behind a stovetop. Decorative backsplash tiles are usually installed like other wall tiles, but the substrate does not have to be waterproof or particularly strong; you can simply tile over any wall surface that is in sound condition. Any type of ceramic or stone tile can be used as long as it is washable. Organic mastic will be strong enough to hold the tiles, but you can use thinset adhesive if you expect the surface to get wet often.

If backsplash tiles butt into a wall cabinet, simply run the field tiles to about $1/8$ inch below the cabinet. Wherever the top edge of the tiles will be exposed, however, use bullnose trim pieces for a finished look. Where backsplash tiles meet the countertop below or a cabinet above, fill the joint with caulk rather than grout to prevent cracking.

You'll probably need to cut tiles to fit around several outlets or switches (see page 69).

plastic laminate postform

- **Postform laminate**
- **Endsplash kit**
- **Iron**
- **Masking tape**
- **Compass**
- **Screws**

Postform tops are lengths of prefabricated plastic laminate on a substrate that come with a rolled front edge and integral coved backsplash. You can find them in various lengths in a limited number of colors at most home improvement stores.

Installing a postform top is as simple as cutting it to size, adding a strip of laminate or wood trim to any exposed ends, and dropping it in place. If you have an L–shaped countertop, you can buy lengths of postform laminate with premitered ends. The ends are glued or bolted

together to form a corner and screwed together on the underside through predrilled holes. If you have walls that are uneven, an easier option for installing your own laminate countertop is to order lengths without a backsplash and use tile or other trim at the wall to hide any gaps.

This project assumes you are installing a top on new base cabinets and installing a drop-in sink. If you are replacing an existing top and will be reusing the sink or other drop-in appliances, trace the shape of the holes that remain after you have removed the appliances from the old top.

1 Measure old top or new base cabinetry as described on page 56. Place the piece of postform upside down on a worktable or sawhorses. Mark off the required length at both the front and back edges of the postform piece. Draw a line between the two marks that will serve as your cutting line. Use a circular saw and scrap guide to cut along the line. Cutting the backsplash can be difficult because it's deeper than the maximum cutting depth of the saw. You'll need to make an additional cut to get through this material.

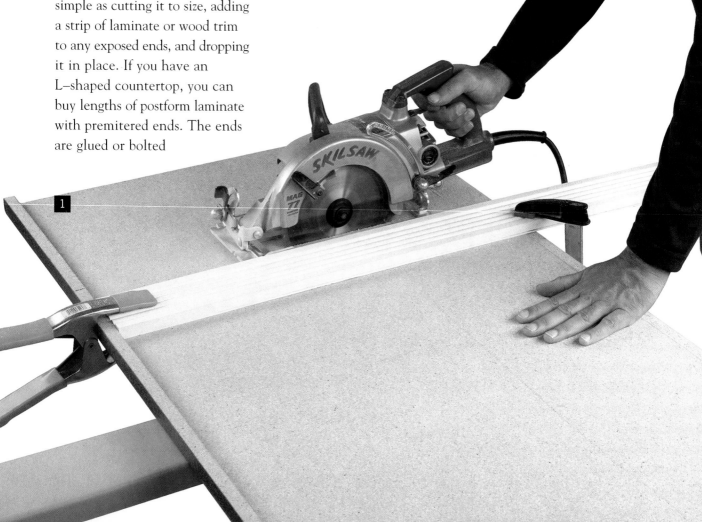

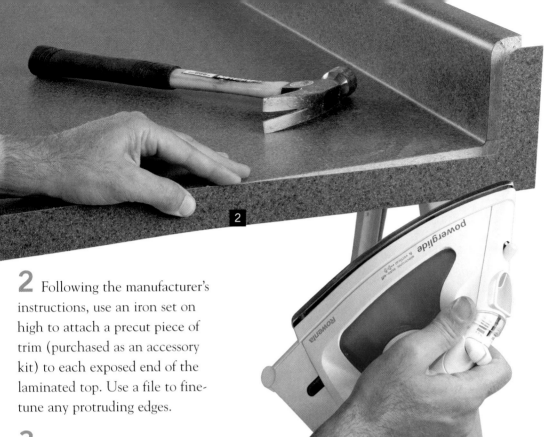

2 Following the manufacturer's instructions, use an iron set on high to attach a precut piece of trim (purchased as an accessory kit) to each exposed end of the laminated top. Use a file to fine-tune any protruding edges.

3 The postform countertop should have a scribing edge along the back of the backsplash that allows you to cut the back of the backsplash to fit tightly against the wall, leaving no gap. If your countertop has no overhang, you would have to contour the entire depth of the splash—a daunting task.

To scribe, run a line of masking tape along the top of the back edge of the backsplash. (This provides a surface for marking and minimizes chipping when cutting.) Position the countertop against the wall, then put a compass and pencil set to the widest gap between the wall and splash. Using this distance, place the pointed end of the compass along the wall and the pencil on the masking tape and run the compass along the length of the backsplash. The pencil will mark the wall's contours on the masking tape.

Remove the counter and use a belt sander, block plane, or saw to shape the splash along the line you marked. Scribing is good for small adjustments. If you have really big gaps, you'll need to cover them with something else, such as a band of tile or wood trim.

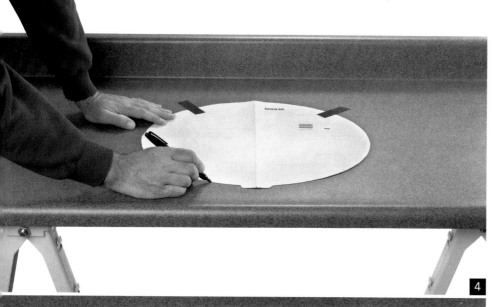

4 Cut out the template that came with your new sink (or the template you made of the old sink hole) and position it on the countertop where the sink will go. Trace around the template. If the sink has no template, turn it upside down on the counter and trace its outline. This will be the outside edge of the sink, so you need to draw a cutting line inside the sink outline.

5 Cut a hole for the sink using a jigsaw. First, drill a pilot hole inside the cutout line that's big enough to slip the blade through. Then start cutting. The edges of the self-rimming sink will cover the cut line, so it doesn't have to be perfectly smooth.

6 Reposition the countertop. Check the top for level—both side to side and front to back— before screwing it down. If you need to make some adjustments, insert wood shims between the cabinet and top. Screw up through the cabinet's corner blocks or stretchers into the countertop. Use screws that will penetrate the countertop but won't poke through its surface. If the top is warped, clamp it down while you secure that spot from below. This will work for small warps only.

laminating a top

- ¾" plywood
- Plastic laminate
- Wood trim
- Masking tape
- Yellow glue
- Multipurpose screws
- Contact cement
- ¼" wooden dowels
- Finishing nails
- Sandpaper
- Water-based varnish
- Laminate roller
- Router with self-piloting trim bit
  or laminate trimmer

There are hundreds of colors and textures of plastic laminate, but very few that are available in prefabricated post-form. The less common colors are expensive to special order, but if you do the job yourself you can save money and get the exact look you want. Plastic laminate is a thin sheet of plastic that is glued down to a substrate. This project uses "shop-grade" hardwood plywood as the substrate. (You can use less expensive medium density fiberboard [MDF] or particleboard; but the latter warps, breaks, and doesn't stand up to water.) We've finished the edges of the top with wood trim. You can apply plastic laminate to the edges, but it can be a tricky procedure.

1 Cut the plywood sheet to your required length and width. In order to make the top thicker than a single sheet of plywood, you'll need to laminate pieces together. You don't need to have a continuous sheet for the bottom layer. Instead, cut two 3- or 4-inch-wide strips of plywood to build up the long edges. Apply yellow glue to the faces of the strips and the underside edges of the top. Then, with all edges flush, secure the strips and plywood sheet together with multipurpose screws; drive the heads flush or just slightly below the surface with a power drill and Phillips-head bit. For added strength, cut the appropriate number of crosspieces to go between the edge strips. Secure them in the same way.

2 Mark cutting lines on the underside of a sheet of plastic laminate so that it measures $\frac{1}{2}$ to 1 inch wider than the length and width of your substrate. (Cutting the sheet a bit oversized will enable you to trim the sheet to fit the substrate.) Lay a length of masking tape along the cutting line you just marked. This makes the line easier to see and also minimizes any chipping. Cut along the line using a table saw, circular saw, or laminate knife.

3 Brush off any dust from the surface of the substrate and clean the top of the substrate and the back of the laminate. Lay both out on a flat surface. Using a paint roller, apply a good coating of contact cement to both surfaces. Let the cement dry to the touch, following the manufacturer's recommendations for drying time.

4 When both surfaces are dry, lay $\frac{1}{4}$-inch wooden dowels evenly every 12 inches along the top of the substrate. These will keep the two materials apart until you have positioned them perfectly. (Once bonded together, you won't be able to pull them apart.) Then carefully lay the sheet of laminate on top of the dowels. This can be done with a helper. Starting at one end, pull the dowels out one at a time to allow each section of laminate to make contact with the substrate. Continue until all dowels are removed and the two surfaces are bonded together.

5 Using a laminate roller, apply pressure to the entire surface of the top to secure the bond and eliminate any air bubbles. Don't expect to fix bulges here; it's probably too late. Roll in all directions to maximize the contact between the laminate and the plywood.

6 Using a router equipped with a self-piloting trim bit or a laminate trimmer, trim all the excess laminate so it is flush with the edge of the top. (You can also use a file set at a slight angle or a sharp block plane.) Whatever trim tool you use, touch up the edges if necessary with a file or a sharp plane.

7 Cut strips of hardwood trim to frame the edges of the top, rounding the top edges with a router for a more finished appearance. Sand them and nail them into the edges with finishing nails. Countersink the nail heads and fill the holes. Sand the wood and finish with a water-based varnish. Immediately wipe away any varnish that gets on the laminate.

wood butcher block

- Metal cart on casters
- Black spray paint
- Masking tape
- Electric drill with $3/16$-inch drill bit and combination countersink-pilot hole bit
- Nine $3/16$-inch U-bolts, each 4 inches long, with 18 nuts
- Twenty-two $1\frac{1}{2}$-by-$1\frac{1}{2}$-inch strips of figured maple, each 40 inches long
- Ten $1/4$-by-$1\frac{1}{2}$-inch strips of English walnut, each 40 inches long
- Carpenter's square
- Router
- Slot cutter for 0mm biscuits (or a plate joiner)
- C-clamps
- Fifty-one 0mm biscuits
- FDA-approved wood glue for cutting boards
- Glue roller
- Pony (pipe) clamps
- Circular saw
- "Maple" wood filler
- 80-, 120-, and 220-grit sandpaper
- Round-over bit
- Eight 2-inch #8 screws
- Heavy mineral oil or oil with wax

I n this project, an inexpensive metal cart from a hardware store becomes the ideal base for a mobile kitchen island. The butcher-block top serves as both a cutting board and serving surface. The lower cart tray stores pots and pans while S-hooks attached to the bottom of the top tray provide hanging storage.

The cart is $36\frac{1}{2}$ inches long by 24 inches wide. For a different size cart, cut the wood strips $3\frac{1}{2}$ inches longer than the cart length. Add or subtract pieces or trim the outer pieces to make the cutting board 1 inch wider than the cart. We recommend you have a cabinet shop cut the maple and walnut strips from the same piece of wood (or two pieces, if necessary).

When you lay out the strips, match the grain lines as much as possible. Even with the thin walnut strips in between, the surface will have visual continuity. On the support pieces (see Step 10), the grain lines do not need to match.

1 Cover the casters on the cart with masking tape. Working outdoors, spray the cart with the black spray paint.

Using the electric drill and $3/16$-inch bit, drill nine holes: three equidistant holes on each long edge and three down the center of the upper tray for the U-bolts that will hold the S-hooks for the hanging pots.

2 Select 18 of the maple pieces for the cutting board and set aside the remaining four pieces for the support frame. Arrange the maple and walnut pieces in a pattern. The outside edges will use two single pieces of maple separated by a ¼-inch width of walnut. In the center, alternate a ¼-inch width of walnut with two pieces of maple set together.

3 Group a section of four maple pieces and any companion walnut strips. Approximately 4 inches from one set of ends, mark a line perpendicular to the lengthwise edges using the carpenter's square. (This side of the pieces will become the underside of the board.) This line is for cutting the first slots for the biscuits (the oval-shaped wafers of compressed wood that fit into the slots to create a tight joint for the maple and walnut pieces).

Keeping the wood pieces together, measure and mark a second line 16 inches from the first line for the center slots. Then mark another line 16 inches from the second line for the slots close to the other end. Repeat this step with the remaining wood strips, grouped in sets of four pieces of maple.

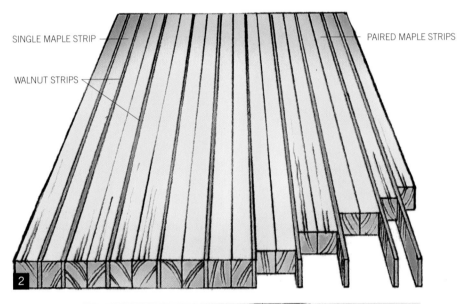

SINGLE MAPLE STRIP

PAIRED MAPLE STRIPS

WALNUT STRIPS

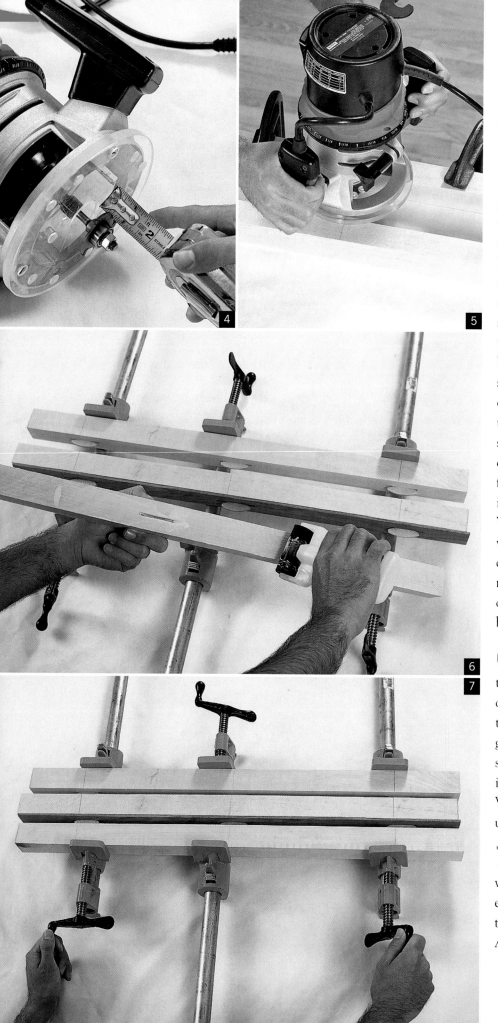

4 On the router, set the slot cutter depth to ⅝ inch, as shown. (Or use a plate joiner.)

5 Clamp the outside maple piece, inside edge up, to your work surface using paper or fabric scraps to protect the wood. Position another piece of maple to support the router, with the marked edge face up to serve as a guideline. (It's essential to keep the router parallel to the piece being cut, not tilted.) Cut three slots for biscuits on the inside edge of the first board, centering them on the marked lines. Cut slots for biscuits on both edges of the remaining pieces, except for the other outside strip, which is cut only on the inside edge. Where a strip of walnut is sandwiched between maple pieces, clamp the walnut strip to one maple piece and cut the two as one strip. Check the fit of the biscuits as you go.

6 Working with a section of the cutting board, that consists of three or four maple pieces and the companion walnut pieces, roll glue sparingly onto the rest of the slotted edges and drip a little glue into the slots. Insert the biscuits. Work efficiently; wood glue sets up quickly.

7 Clamp the pieces together with the pony clamps, applying even pressure. Use dry paper towels to wipe off the excess glue. Allow the glue to dry as specified in the manufacturer's instructions. Repeat Steps 6 and 7 with the remaining sections of maple and walnut strips. Glue and clamp all the sections together.

8 Measure and mark the board to $37\frac{1}{2}$ inches (or your finished length, if it is different). Trim the ends with the circular saw. Fill any imperfections or nicks on the side of the board that will be exposed with the maple-colored wood filler. Allow filler to dry.

Sand the facing side of the board, starting with the 80-grit sandpaper, and following with the 120- and 220-grit sandpaper. Using the router with the round-over bit, finish the edges, rounding the corners if desired.

9 Measure the length and width of the cart tray's interior. If there are obstacles, such as screws protruding through the sides, take the measurements *inside* these obstacles so the support frame will sit inside them. Draw a rectangle to these measurements on the underside of the board, carefully positioning it so the board will overhang the cart by the same distance on all four sides.

10 To make the support frame, cut the four remaining pieces of maple to the lengths of the drawn lines less 3 inches. Position the support pieces so their outside edges are on the drawn lines.

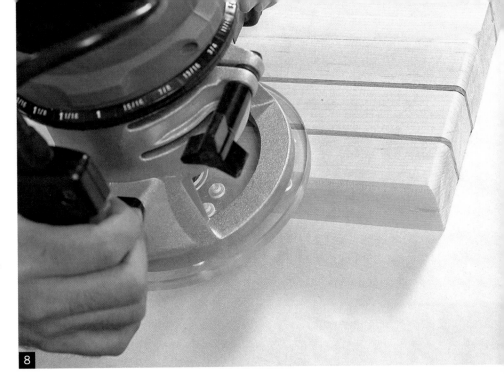

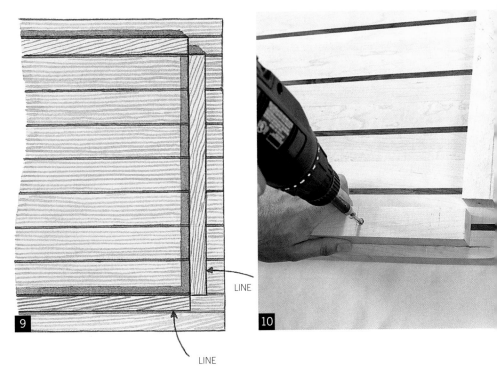

LINE

LINE

Using the #8 screws and the combination countersink-pilot hole bit, screw the support pieces to the board. Apply heavy mineral oil (or a butcher-block oil with wax) to the exposed face of the board with a clean rag.

To attach the U-bolts that will hold the S-hooks for pots and pans, thread a nut onto a bolt. Insert the bolt from the top side into the holes you drilled through the cart tray in Step 1; thread another nut onto the bolt and tighten. Repeat for each bolt. Set the board into the tray.

glass desktop

- Four 2 × 3 lengths of hardwood cut to 28¼" for legs
- 2 × 2 hardwood for frame, cut to desired width and length
- Sheet of glass
- Nails or 2" brads
- Wood plugs (same or contrasting hardwood)
- Power nailer
- Screws
- Wood glue
- Square
- Clamp

Glass can be mounted as a top in ultra-modern or traditional base designs. The more modern installations that involve stainless-steel bolts or brackets require special skills and tools that are best left to professionals. This desktop is a relatively easy do-it-yourself project for homeowners and creates a sleek, contemporary surface. If the maximum length of your desktop is 4 feet, you should not need cross supports under the glass. We recommend using either ¼-inch-thick tempered glass or ⅜-inch untempered. Order the glass after you have made the frame, so you can give exact finished measurements. It is very important that you create a perfectly square frame so the glass will fit. Allow five to seven days for the glass to be cut and edge-polished.

1 Cut four lengths of 2 by 3 to 28¼ inches to serve as the legs of the table. Using a router, shape a rabbet in the top of each leg ¾ inch deep by 1½ inches wide, or the depth of your top frame. This will serve as a ledge that the table frame will sit on.

Next, cut two pieces of 2 by 2 several inches longer than the desired length of the desktop. Cut two more pieces several inches wider than the desired width. (You will be mitering the ends after rabbeting.)

2 Using a router, cut a ½-inch wide rabbet along the entire length of each of the pieces of wood to the depth of the glass you will be using. Check each piece to make sure the rabbet is exactly ¼ inch or ⅜ inch deep so that the glass sits flush with the top of the wood frame. Miter the ends of each piece to the desired length.

3 Join the sides and fronts of the frame together by first spreading glue on each piece. Then hold the miter joint tight in one hand and shoot 2-inch brads into it using a power nailer. (It is very difficult to make a clean miter joint using hand tools, so this technique is recommended.) Measure the frame to ensure that it is perfectly square. If not, make adjustments so it is.

5 clamp it in place. Check that it is completely vertical with a square. Drill smaller pilot holes through both the leg and frame. Drive screws to secure each joint. Sink the screws far enough so that you can cover them with wood plugs. Repeat with the other three legs. Spread glue in screw holes and insert wood plugs. Let the glue dry overnight and then sand the plugs flush with the surface. Finish all the inside and outside edges of the table frame with paint, stain, or clear varnish.

6 Measure the inset in the frame and order a sheet of glass. Set the glass into the frame.

4 Sand the frame, then place it upside down on a flat surface. Drill countersink holes for screw heads in the legs.

5 Working on one leg at a time, spread wood glue along its rabbet, attach the leg to the frame about 3 inches in from its edge, and

COOL TABLETOP

A back-painted glass top is a quick, simple, high-impact way to add a splash of color to any room. Have a piece of glass cut to size; then use a large foam brush to paint the underside. We used ¼-inch plate glass with a flat polished edge and sky blue latex paint, which looks greener through the glass. If you don't like the color, simply hose off the paint and try a different one.

zinc-topped serving counter

- 2 × 4 fir
- 1 × 6 fir (for bottom shelf)
- 1 × 4 fir (for bottom shelf)
- Yellow glue
- ¾" exterior-grade sheet of plywood
- Zinc sleeve
- Router with roundover bit or table saw with dado blade
- Clamps
- Screws
- Sandpaper
- Nails

A freestanding patio serving counter is ideal for out-door entertaining. When equipped with a zinc top, it is weatherproof as well as easy to clean and maintain. Build the sturdy wooden base first and then order the zinc sleeve to fit over a plywood substrate. Our measurements are for a 5-foot long top.

You can adjust the measurements to fit your particular needs.

1 Cut 8 lengths of 2 by 4 to 32 inches to make the legs. Using a router or a table saw with a dado blade, cut a rabbet ¾-inch deep by 3 inches wide at the top of each board. Then cut a dado ¾-inch deep by 3 inches wide,

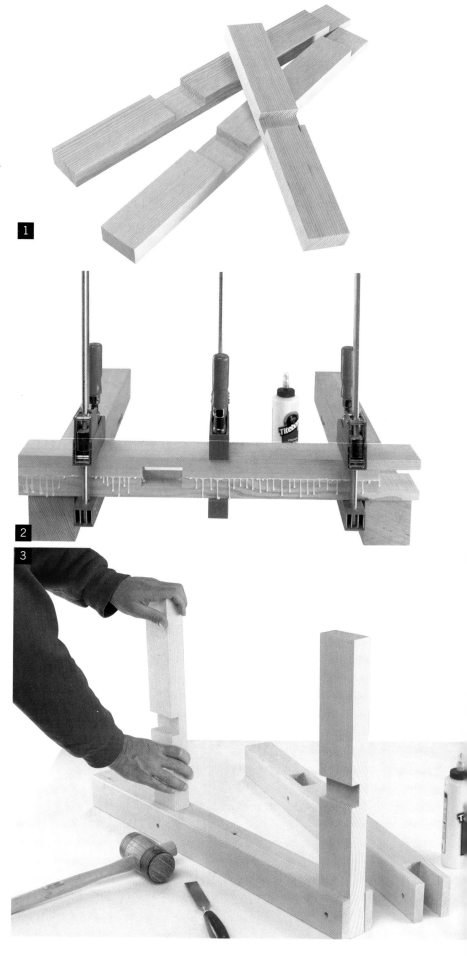

8 inches from the bottom of each board, on the same side as the rabbet. Rip both edges to get rid of the rounded factory edges so that the finished width is 3 inches. When the pairs of ripped 2 by 4s are assembled, each leg will be 3 inches square.

2 Make four leg "sandwiches" by taking pairs of notched 2 by 4s and gluing them together, with their notches facing each other. First make sure the notches of each pair align perfectly, so there is an opening at the top of each leg and a mortise near the bottom. Then use a lot of yellow glue and clamp each assembly together. Let dry overnight. The next day, sand away any excess glue and make sure all seams are flush. Using a router and round-over bit, round the four outside edges of each leg.

3 Next, cut four lengths of 2 by 4 to 20 inches long for the cross-rungs. Rip the crossrungs to 3 inches wide. Cut a ¾-inch-deep by 1½-inches-wide dado in the center of each of the boards. Put one leg, notch facing up, on a flat surface. Then insert a crossrung, with the dado facing sideways, in the mortise until it bottoms out. Insert another crossrung into the top notch so it's flush with the outside edges of the leg. Add the second leg on the opposite ends of the crossrungs.

4 Check to make sure all is square. Then remove the crossrungs, spread glue inside the notches, reinsert the boards, and screw the assembly together.

5 Top and bottom stretchers will tie the two side leg assemblies together. Cut two lengths of 2-by-4 stretchers to 53 inches. Rip the boards to 1½ inches by 3 inches wide. Spread glue in the bottom dadoes of each side assembly. Insert the bottom stretcher into each dado and screw the pieces together. Repeat the process to attach top stretcher.

6 Cut one 1-by-6 board and two 1-by-4 boards to 54½ inches long. Space them across the inside of the bottom frame of the table. Nail them in place.

4

7 Cut a sheet of plywood to 22 inches by 60 inches (or the distance between the outside edges of the four legs, plus an inch or two for an overhang). Center the plywood on top of the base and secure it to the legs with wood screws. Order the zinc top from a sheet metal fabricator. Its inside measurement should be the width and length of the plywood. The sides should be 2 inches deep. Press the zinc onto the plywood, using a rubber mallet to tap it in place, if necessary.

5   6

finishing a wood countertop

Plywood, recycled wood slabs, or a solid-core wood door can be used to create a work surface or countertop. Depending on how the surface will be used, you can finish it with wood stain, sealer, paint, or varnish; varnish can be used alone or applied over a color stain or paint to protect the surface. Use only water-based, non-toxic products for any surface that will be used to prepare food. Repair any surface flaws and sand before applying one of the following finishes.

PIGMENTED STAIN

Most pigmented stains are simple to apply. Gel stains are easier to work with than liquids, and seem to go on a little more evenly.

Using a rag, apply liquid or gel pigmented stain straight from the can. Once the surface is covered with the stain, use a clean, soft cloth to remove excess and buff out the surface, following the wood grain. Some stains get more intense the longer they stay on before you wipe them out. Some can be lightened by rubbing harder. If the first coat is too light, add a second one. Let the stain dry overnight.

WATER STAIN

Water stains are more transparent than pigments. They come in wood tones as well as intense colors such as red, green, and blue. Water-based aniline dyes are sold in dry form. Mix the powdered dye with warm water or alcohol in a jar, following the manufacturer's directions.

Other water stains come pre-mixed. Since water stains can raise wood grain, rub plain water on the surface first and then sand back the resulting "fuzzies" before staining.

Use either a disposable foam brush or rag to apply the water stain. The stain will soak into the wood after it's applied, so plan to put it on quickly and have a soft, absorbent cloth ready to remove the excess. Rub the cloth softly across the wood with the grain, turning it over frequently. Don't rub hard because you'll scuff up the grain. Soft woods will soak up more color than hard ones.

If necessary, put on a second coat of color right after buffing the first. Let the stain dry overnight. If the stain raised the wood grain, use fine sandpaper or a finishing pad to smooth it down lightly.

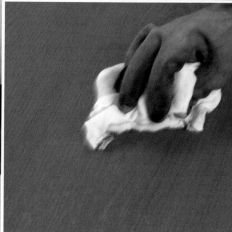

PENETRATING OIL

Antique oils, penetrating resins, and tung oils are penetrating oils (actually, oil-varnish blends). These finishes are easy to apply.

You can use a rag or a brush to apply penetrating oil, or simply pour it directly from the can and spread it around with a rag or brush. The wood will drink up a lot of the first coat.

Let the oil sit for the prescribed amount of time (usually around 15 minutes) and then buff off any excess with a clean, soft rag. If you leave the oil on too long, it will turn sticky and won't dry. Since these oils aren't surface films, you have to apply numerous thin coats if you want to build up some luster.

WATER-BASE VARNISH

The new water-base varnishes are a lot easier to clean up and dry faster. They look milky when first applied but dry to a clear finish. A water-base finish requires two coats minimum, but three or even four is usually better.

Use either a good synthetic-bristle or foam brush to apply each coat. Flow on a liberal coat with the brush and then "top off" the varnish, making light strokes with the grain using just the tip of the brush.

Once the varnish is dry (two to four hours), lightly sand the surface with 200-grit paper to remove dust nibs and any raised grain. Apply a second coat, wait, sand, and apply a third coat, if necessary. After the final coat, rub out the finish with a clean, soft cloth.

ENAMEL PAINT

Before painting wood, first apply an undercoat or primer to seal the wood. Let the primer dry, then smooth the surface using 220-grit sandpaper.

Next, brush the enamel paint generously on the wood and then feather it out with lighter strokes in the direction of the grain. For larger areas, use a 3-inch paint roller or a paint pad, then smooth out the finish with a paint brush using light brush strokes.

Let this coat dry and then sand lightly with 320- or 400-grit paper before applying a second and final coat. For the ultimate in gloss and protection, apply a coat or two of clear varnish.

indoor concrete counter

- Blue painter's tape
- Plastic sheets
- Kraft paper
- Large fan
- Eye and ear protection
- Respirator
- Heavy-duty leather or synthetic gloves
- Right-angle grinder
- 1-pound coffee can
- Portland cement, gray and white
- 90-mesh sand
- Concrete polymer
- One 1-gallon bucket and two 5-gallon buckets
- Electric drill with mixing paddle bit
- 2½-by-12-inch cement finishing trowel
- Heavy-duty rubber or latex gloves
- Spray bottle with fine-mist nozzle
- 220-grit sandpaper
- "Sandstone" concentrated concrete stain
- 2-inch paintbrush
- Tile sponge
- Water-based sealer

This project provides an inexpensive and attractive way to transform an old tile countertop without removing it. By covering old tile with concrete enhanced by a polymer, you can create a surface that is as durable as it is striking. Our project involves mixing the concrete by combining cement, sand, concrete polymer, and water. You can also purchase premeasured concrete countertop mixes in designer colors that may be even more scratch and crack resistant. See Resources on page 125 for more information.

Since typical bags of concrete may contain more than you'll need, look for a supplier who will sell you smaller quantities. Each batch of concrete will cover approximately 65 square feet. Remember to include the backsplash in your square footage calculation.

1 Remove the switch plates and outlet covers on the backsplash; cover the openings with blue painter's tape. Protect the cabinets with plastic sheets and the floor with kraft paper.

Open all the windows and doors and place the fan where it will push the air through the room and outdoors. Put on the eye protection, ear protection, respirator, and heavy-duty gloves; the respirator is a must because of the tile dust that will be stirred up. Holding the grinder at a 30-degree angle, rough up the surface of the tile so it will accept the wet concrete.

2 Rough up the corners and other spots you can't reach with the grinder with the claw end of a hammer.

Using the 1-pound coffee can as a measure, premix two cans of white cement and one-sixth can of gray cement in the 1-gallon bucket. Stir the mixture to blend thoroughly.

3 Combine two cans of the premixed cement from the previous step (discard the leftover) and two cans of 90-mesh sand in a 5-gallon bucket, then stir to blend thoroughly. In the other 5-gallon bucket, combine one can of concrete polymer and one can of water. Add the dry ingredients to the liquid and mix for several minutes until the consistency is smooth. Use your electric drill with the mixing paddle bit.

4 Put on gloves and spread the concrete over the tile backsplash using the cement finishing trowel. Work in 2- to 3-foot sections, trailing off the edges to avoid buildup where you stop and start. If the concrete is too thick and won't adhere to the backsplash, let the mixture rest in the bucket until it sets up a little—the concrete has an "open" (workable) time of approximately 15 minutes. If the mixture seems too thick at any time, spray a fine mist of water on the concrete on the backsplash with the spray bottle. Make the surface as smooth as possible but don't attempt to cover the tile or fill the grout lines completely with this application; this is merely a base coat.

5 Trowel a base coat of concrete onto the countertop deck using the technique in Step 4.

6 To apply the concrete to the edge, load the trowel and hold it parallel to the countertop just below the lower edge of the tile trim, with the flat side of the trowel blade facing up.

7 Roll the trowel up and over the edge, coating the trim surface evenly. If your trim has a square edge, hold the trowel at an angle against the trim and drag the trowel upward without rolling it over the edge. The temperature and humidity will affect the drying time. Err on the side of safety and let the concrete dry overnight. Allow any leftover concrete to set up in the bucket until it's firm enough to hold together. Turn the bucket upside down to release the concrete, then break it apart to make it easier to dispose of.

8 Once the first coat is dry, sand down rough spots using the 220-grit sandpaper. Spray the surface with a fine mist of water in order to help the second coat adhere to the base coat.

9 Mix a second batch of concrete according to the instructions in Step 3. Trowel a second coat onto the backsplash as you did the first, working to cover the surface more completely this time. Trowel a second coat onto the countertop deck.

10 Trowel a second coat over the edge. To round the edge, use part of a plastic milk jug or a coffee can lid, bending and pulling it toward you as shown. The polymer makes the mixture sticky, like white glue. If it seems too sticky and the plastic doesn't glide smoothly, spray the concrete with just enough water to give the surface a sheen and continue working. If the concrete is too wet, allow it to dry a little before continuing.

Allow the second coat to dry; sand if needed. Apply a third coat to the backsplash, deck, and edge if needed. Allow to dry; sand.

11 Mix the concentrated concrete stain in a glass bowl not used for food in a ratio of 1 part stain to 10 parts water. Don't be alarmed that the color of the stain is not what you expect: the mineral salts in the stain, which is acidic, will react chemically with the cement to bring up the color.

Before applying the stain to the surface, experiment with a scrap of dried concrete to find the stain-to-water ratio that you like. If you add more water, the surface will have a subtle patina. Use less and the color will be more intense.

Cover the deck with plastic and place a bucket of fresh water nearby. Put on the rubber or latex gloves. With just a little bit of stain on your paintbrush, apply it to the backsplash in a circular motion. Remove the plastic and apply the stain to the deck, then

to the edging. Be sure not to drip on the surface—drips can't be wiped up and will leave prominent, permanent marks. Have a helper work alongside you to wipe off excess stain with a tile sponge, rinsing the sponge often.

After 48 hours, wipe down the surface with a damp sponge to remove any residue. Following the manufacturer's instructions, seal the backsplash and deck with the water-based sealer.

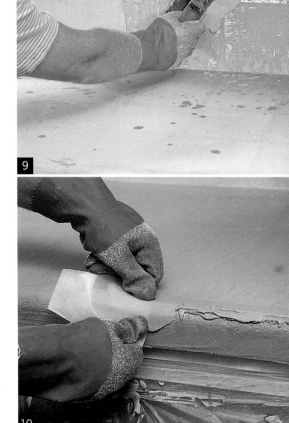

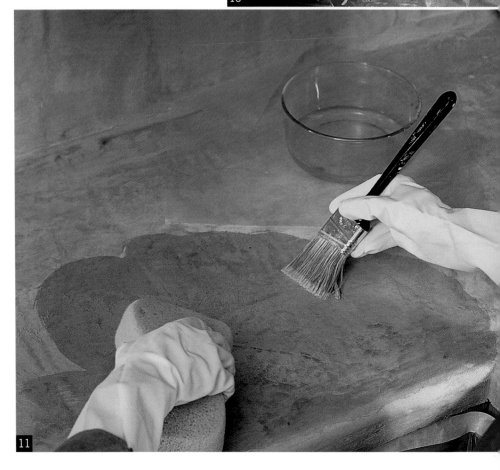

outdoor concrete countertop

- 2-by-4 pine for frame
- 2-by-6 pine for frame
- Backerboard
- Clamps
- 2 sheets stucco lath the size of the countertop
- Silicone caulk
- Concrete mix
- Concrete colorant
- Magnesium or wood float
- 2 by 4 for screeding
- Concrete edger
- Magnesium trowel
- Steel trowel

Building an indoor concrete countertop takes experience and skill. If you're willing to experiment, there are companies that sell kits that include concrete mixes with additives as well as complete instruction manuals.

For those who want to tackle a concrete project that requires a little less experience, this poured-in-place outdoor countertop is easier to make. Any imperfections in the finish will look more natural in the outdoors.

This finished unit includes a built-in barbecue. Note: An outdoor counter made of concrete or other heavy materials must rest on a solid concrete footing.

1 Cut a sheet of backerboard to fit flush with the countertop base. Attach backerboard to base. Cut a 2 by 4 to fit snugly around the backerboard. Position pieces of 2 by 4 with their top edges flush with the top of the backerboard and nail them into the backerboard; also nail them together at each corner. (This 2-by-4 frame is used to create a 1½-inch overhang beyond the base when the frame is removed.)

2 Cut pieces of 2 by 6 to fit around the 2-by-4 frame. Position the 2 by 6 so its bottom edge is flush with the bottom edge of the

CONCRETE TIPS

Poured-in-place countertops may be easier to make than those poured into a mold, but they are notorious for developing cracks. To minimize cracking, take at least some of these precautions.

PURCHASE HIGH-STRENGTH CONCRETE. If you are ordering ready-mix, get a seven-bag mix, which has extra Portland cement. If you use dry-mix bags, purchase "high early" concrete.

MAKE A VERY STIFF MIX. Add only as much water as necessary to ensure the mix is completely wet. The thinner the mix, the more likely it is to crack.

USE METAL REINFORCEMENT. It will not stop tiny cracks, but it will keep the cracks from enlarging.

ADD FIBER REINFORCEMENT. This is available from concrete suppliers. The fibers stop small cracks, but they make it difficult to finish the top. One solution is to add fibers only to the first part of the mix.

2 by 4 and nail it in place. This will be the main frame and result in a top that is approximately 2½ inches above the backerboard. The total countertop thickness, including the backerboard, will be about 3 inches. Support the frame with temporary vertical boards and use a clamp or two to hold the frame firmly together.

3 Cut stucco lath to fit so that it comes to about an inch from the perimeter of the frame. Do not oil the frame; doing so may change the concrete's color at the edges. Apply silicone caulk to seal any gaps. At the corners, apply a bead of caulk to help round the edges.

4 Experiment with concrete colors until you achieve a mix you like. (Remember, wet concrete is darker than cured concrete.) Develop a precise recipe using a bathroom scale or measuring cup to ensure that you add the correct amount of colorant to each batch of concrete you mix. Take care to make the mix as dry as possible; it should be completely wet but not pourable. You can strengthen the countertop with fiber reinforcement if you like.

5 Wipe the formed area with a wet rag to ensure good adhesion to the backerboard. To minimize spatters, shovel the concrete into a bucket, then pour from the bucket into the form. Pour the first batch into the center of the formed area.

6 Use a board or a float to move and spread the concrete so that it is about half as thick as the height of the frame. Set the stucco lath on top of the concrete and add more concrete. Spread the concrete, pushing downward and tamping it to prevent voids and bubbles. If the forms bulge, pull them in straight with bar clamps set across the forms.

Continue filling and spreading concrete. Add small amounts at a time to fill any low spots. If larger pieces of aggregate sit on the top, remove them and fill in the holes. Push the concrete firmly against the form at the perimeter. Then spread the concrete with a magnesium or wood float. Finally, use a piece of 2 by 4 to screed the top so that it is level with the tops of the form boards.

7 Lightly tap the sides of the form with a hammer to remove small air pockets.

8 As soon as any bleed water disappears, run a magnesium float across the surface to begin smoothing. Press just hard enough to bring up a little bleed water.

9 Run a concrete edger along the perimeter two or three times until the surface is smooth. As soon as the bleed water disappears, run a magnesium trowel over the surface to further smooth it. Let the concrete dry. In hot or dry weather, cover the surface with plastic to slow down the curing

process and increase the hardness of the concrete.

10 When the concrete seems hard enough to hold its shape, carefully release the squeeze clamps one at a time. If the concrete forces the form outward when you do this, tighten the clamp again and let the concrete dry longer. Once all the clamps are off, unfasten the form boards and gently pull them away.

11 Use a magnesium trowel to smooth the edges of the slab. If any large gaps are present, fill them by hand and trowel it again.

12 Use a small piece of plastic to smooth and round off the corners and edges.

13 Go over the surface with a steel trowel; a pool trowel like the one shown is easier for beginners. Avoid overworking the surface. If troweling starts to roughen rather than to smooth the surface, it is time to stop.

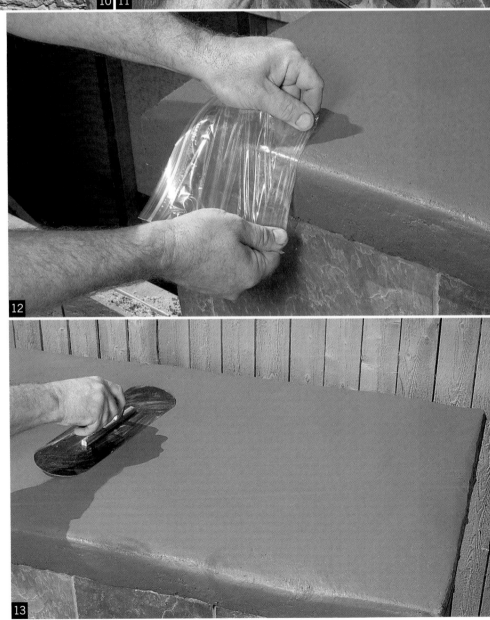

potting table with sink

- Lumber (see cutting list)
- Deck screws
- Stainless steel bar sink (optional)
- Large galvanized cup hooks
- Clear varnish (optional)
- Jigsaw

CUTTING LIST

Dimension	Cut Length	Quantity
2 × 4	53¼"	2 (back legs)
2 × 4	33¼"	2 (front legs)
1 × 4	47"	4 (front & back stretchers)
1 × 4	22"	4 (side crossrungs)
1 × 6	48"	4 (lower shelf slats)
1 × 6	48"	4 (top shelf slats)
1 × 4	22"	2 (sink braces)
1 × 4	47"	1 (rail)
1 × 6	48"	1 (top of rail)

A potting table gives you a space to start, divide, and repot plants, mix soil, and water seedlings. Construction-heart redwood and cedar are the best materials to use for this project. This table has a cutout for a stainless steel sink, which you can drop in place. Note: Predrill pilot holes before driving screws near edges to avoid splitting.

1 Each side of the table base is made from two 2-by-4 legs and two 1-by-4 crossrungs. The front 2-by-4s are at bench height; the rear ones stick up to support a back shelf and tool rail. First, lay down a set of front and back legs on a flat surface and set the first 1-by-4 side crossrung on top of the legs 6 inches from their even

ends. Attach the pieces with screws. Lay another side crossrung across the legs flush with the top of the front leg and screw together. Repeat with the second set of front and back legs.

2 Use screws to tie the two side assemblies together with 1-by-4 stretchers across the front and back. The stretchers should be positioned at the same height as the crossrungs.

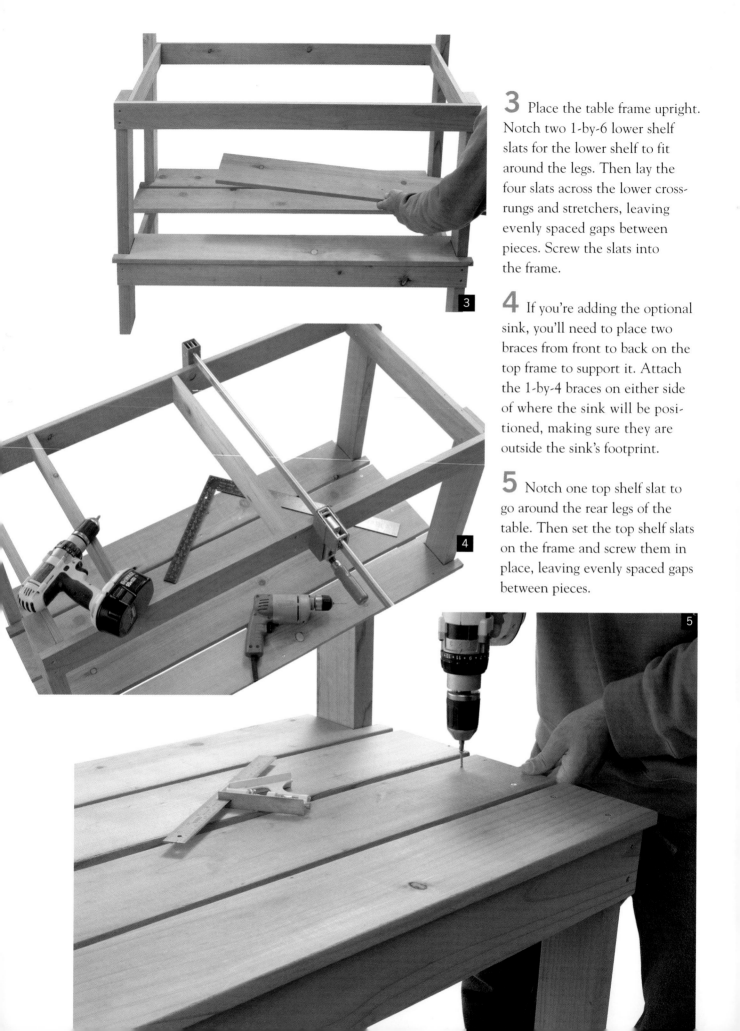

3 Place the table frame upright. Notch two 1-by-6 lower shelf slats for the lower shelf to fit around the legs. Then lay the four slats across the lower cross-rungs and stretchers, leaving evenly spaced gaps between pieces. Screw the slats into the frame.

4 If you're adding the optional sink, you'll need to place two braces from front to back on the top frame to support it. Attach the 1-by-4 braces on either side of where the sink will be positioned, making sure they are outside the sink's footprint.

5 Notch one top shelf slat to go around the rear legs of the table. Then set the top shelf slats on the frame and screw them in place, leaving evenly spaced gaps between pieces.

6 Place the sink upside down on the top shelf, making sure it is between the support braces underneath the top. Trace around its outside edges with chalk or an erasable pencil. Measure the lip and use this distance to draw a second line inside the one you traced. This will be your cutting line. Use a jigsaw to cut the hole for the sink. Set the sink in place. Attach a drain hose to sink, if necessary.

7 Attach the final piece of 1 by 6 horizontally across the top of the rail. Then align a 1-by-4 rail with the top edges of the rear legs and screw it in place. Screw a number of large galvanized cup hooks into the rail to hold potting tools. You can finish the table with clear varnish or let it age gracefully.

craft table

- Self-healing vinyl board cover (available from art and drafting supply stores or www.charrette.com)
- Hollow-core door
- Two paintbrushes
- Primer (optional)
- Satin latex paint
- Two sawhorses
- Double-sided tape for vinyl board cover
- Craft knife
- Metal ruler
- Pencil
- Small number stencils
- Masking tape
- Stencil paint
- Stencil paintbrush
- Heavy paper or chipboard

While the kitchen or dining room table often serves double duty as a craft table, it is not designed for this function. This is an easy-to-construct craft table that gives you a surface you can cut on without damaging it; it also provides a built-in tape measure. The table is large enough to handle sewing projects and can be dismantled easily.

The base consists of two adjustable sawhorses—because counter height is more convenient for some tasks and desk height is better for others—but any sturdy sawhorses will do. The top is a birch hollow-core door with a flat surface.

To create a smooth and durable drawing and cutting surface, we covered the door with self-healing vinyl board cover. The board cover, which comes in a variety of widths and lengths, is available from art and drafting supply stores. The closer you can get the board cover to the exact size of your door, the better.

We stenciled a basic measuring system onto the board cover so that general measurements can be made without a measuring stick.

1 Unroll the board cover on a flat surface and weight with books for several hours to smooth out.

Prime the edges of the door if necessary. Apply one or two coats of satin latex paint to the sawhorses and to door edges.

Lay the door flat. Without removing the protective strip, apply double-sided tape in continuous lines along all four edges of the top surface of the door, as close to the edges as possible. Run several additional strips of tape down the length of the middle of the door.

Align the board cover with the top of the door. Remove the protective strip from the tape at one long edge and adhere the board cover. Moving from one side of the door to the other, remove the protective strip from the double-sided tape and smooth the board cover onto the door. Trim any board cover that overhangs the edges of the door with a craft knife and a metal ruler. Weight the surface to ensure good adhesion.

2 To create a measuring line on the surface of the board cover, start measuring from one edge of the table and use a pencil and ruler to create ¹/₂-inch-long tick marks at 1-foot increments. Center number stencils (1 through 6, respectively) above each tick mark. (Note that the stencils in the corners of the door cannot be centered on the tick marks. In these instances, place the stencil to one side of the mark.)

Secure with masking tape. Using a circular motion, swirl a stencil brush in the stencil paint. After rubbing the bristles over a paper towel so the brush is not dripping with paint, lightly press the brush into the stencil cutout, making the paint as translucent or opaque as you want.

3 To highlight the tick marks themselves, create a stencil by cutting a ¹/₁₆-by-¹/₂-inch rectangle out of a piece of heavy paper or chipboard. Center your stencil on each of the penciled tick marks and follow the stencil painting instructions outlined above.

For a quick and easy alternative to the stenciled measuring system, adhere a tape measure to one edge of the door.

folding workbench

- Five 8-foot lengths of 1-by-6 pine
- 1½-inch finishing nails
- Two 8-foot lengths of 1-by-2 pine
- One 4-foot-square sheet of ⅛-inch pegboard
- 4-inch headed nails
- One 4-by-8-foot sheet of ¾-inch plywood
- One 8-foot length of 2-by-4 Douglas fir
- #8 flathead wood screws
- Four 5-inch T-hinges
- Two 10-inch double-arm lid supports
- One latching hasp

CUTTING LIST FOR 1-BY-6 PINE

Cut Length	Quantity
70½ inches	2
37½ inches	2
36¾ inches	1
36 inches	4
6 inches	4

If you have the space in your garage or workshop, you can attach a recycled solid wood door or sheet of medium-density fiberboard to sawhorses to create a permanent workbench. For those with space constraints, this 72-inch-long folding workbench gives you a large, durable surface you can pull down or hide away as needed. When open, it requires a 46-inch depth clearance. When closed, it projects only 8 inches from the wall. You can change the depth to suit your storage needs.

1 Start by butt-joining the two 37½-inch boards onto the two 70½-inch boards to create a rec-tangular box with outside dimensions of 37½ by 72 inches. Nail the boards together with 1½-inch finishing nails. Nail one 6-inch board into the center of one 36-inch shelf board. Set this into the box so that the long board butts into a short side of the box and the 6-inch board butts into a long side of the box. Nail through the outside of the box into the edges of both boards.

2 Set the 36¾-inch board on end in the box and butt it up against the 36-inch shelf. Nail through the outside of the box into this center divider. Stand the box frame up on a flat surface, with the shelves on the left, and

repeat the process of nailing the 6-inch boards into the 36-inch shelves and installing them in the left side of the box. Work until you have four shelves in place.

3 Next, nail the sheet of pegboard to the back of the right side of the box. Cut two 72-inch-long furring strips from the 1-by-2 pine. Nail one of them to the back top of the box frame so that the bottom of the strip is flush with the back top edge of the frame board. The strip will extend above the frame by ¾ inch.

4 Mark the wall in several places about 35¼ inches above the floor. Draw a level line along these marks. Mark the location of studs just above this line as well as 40 inches above it. Position the top of the second furring strip along the line and nail it into the studs using 4-inch headed nails.

5 Rest the bottom of the box on top of the furring strip, place it against the wall, and nail the top furring strip into the studs above the top of the box. Nail the box to the lower furring strip.

6 Cut two pieces of 2 by 4 to 36 inches to serve as legs. Mount them to one long side of the 4-by-8-foot sheet of ¾-inch plywood (the tabletop work surface) 8 inches in from both sides and 2 inches in from the front; use T-hinges. Secure them with #8 flathead wood screws. Mount the lid supports (used to hold the legs at a 90-degree angle when the tabletop is open) 7 inches from the top of the legs and ⅜ inch in from the outside back edges of the legs. Screw the

stems of the other two T-hinges to the top back edge of the tabletop 8 inches in from the sides.

7 Butt the plywood tabletop to the bottom edge of the box and attach the T-hinges to the bottom shelf. Attach the latching hasp to the underside of the table and to the frame at the top to hold the table closed vertically when not in use.

repairs and maintenance

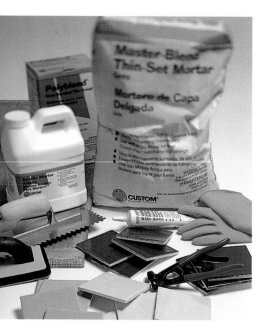

A work surface gets more use and abuse than almost any other structural element in your home. Proper maintenance is critical to keep surfaces in good working order. The best products to use (or not use) to maintain each type of surface are provided at the end of the chapter.

Even with the most careful maintenance, some materials will sustain damage and require repairs. On the following pages we include information on how to repair minor blemishes on tile, plastic laminate, wood, solid surfaces, metal, and stone. More serious damage may require professional assistance or replacement.

Most minor damage to countertops is cosmetic—it will affect the look but not the usefulness of the work surface. If you are not bothered by slight imperfections, you can disguise most small scratches, dents, and burns by placing an attractive bowl or decorative object strategically over the mark. If you use a surface to prepare food, however, be aware that cracks and gouges in many porous materials can harbor bacteria and should be repaired.

tile repair

When a section of grout is dislodged or a tile cracks, you don't have to replace the entire work surface. Grout can be cleaned and repaired relatively easily. Broken tiles can be removed and replaced.

The hardest part of the job is finding a new tile and new grout in colors that match the old. Tile colors will change from one manufacturer to another and sometimes from one box of tiles to another—especially if you're dealing with natural stone. A subtle difference in color can be dramatic once the new tile is installed.

If you're lucky, you'll have a few surplus tiles and a bit of grout from the original surface in storage. If not, and the manufacturer's name is printed on the back of the damaged tile, you can do most of your hunting by calling suppliers. The alternative is to take the old tile to tile dealers and look for a new one that matches.

Grout can be even more difficult to match. Even if you get the correct brand and color, chances are that your existing grout has darkened slightly after years of use. Clean it before you make any repairs. Chip off a piece of the clean grout and take it to a tile dealer. Look for the grout sample that comes closest to what you have installed.

CLEANING GROUT

Sometimes just cleaning the grout is enough to give new life to an older countertop. It also is essential before regrouting any damaged area. First, spray on a commercial grout cleaner or a solution of $\frac{1}{4}$ cup chlorine bleach to 1 quart of warm water for white grout. Let the cleaner soak in for a few minutes. Then, scrub it with a bristle brush or a fiberglass mesh pad. Rinse the area clean and let it dry. Whenever you clean grout, reapply a grout sealer.

REGROUTING TILE

If you see even a small hole in the grout, patch it right away, before moisture has a chance to work its way below the tiles. Mix a small batch of grout. Press it in with your finger. Wipe away the excess, allow it to dry, and clean the area with a wet sponge.

If grout is recessed, applying a thin coat of grout on top of it is risky; there's a good chance that the new grout will flake off eventually. It's safest to take out all the grout with a grout saw before regrouting.

Removing grout is painstaking work, but well worth the effort. Saw with slow, deliberate strokes to avoid damaging any tiles. Apply only moderate pressure; let the grout saw do most of the work. If the going starts to get slow, the saw may have become dull; buy another one. If you have a lot of grout to remove, consider buying an electric grout-removal tool.

After the grout is removed, vacuum away all dust and wipe the area with a wet sponge. For complete instructions on applying new grout, see page 65.

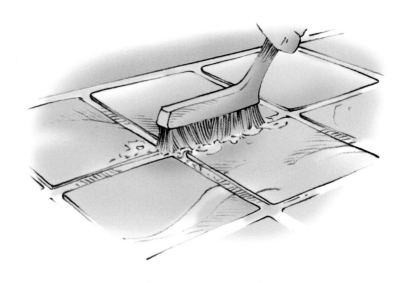

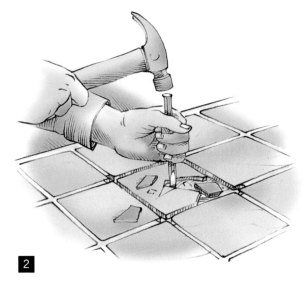

1

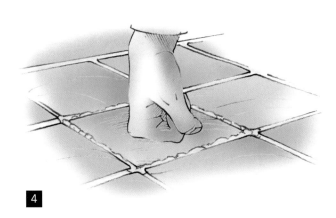

2

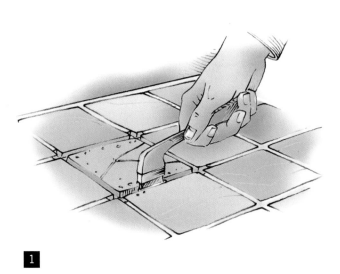

3

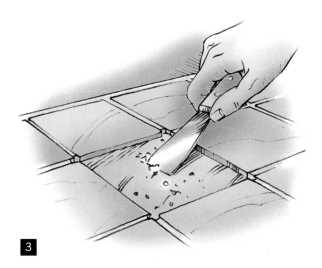

4

REPLACING CRACKED TILE

To remove and replace a cracked tile, you need a grout saw, a hammer, and a putty knife or chisel.

1 First, use the grout saw to remove the grout all around the tile.

2 Then, tap on the cracked tile with a chisel and hammer until the tile breaks apart. Be careful not to damage any of the the surrounding tiles.

3 Using a putty knife or chisel, remove the pieces of broken tile as well as the old adhesive and any remaining grout. Vacuum or dust the area to create a clean substrate for the new tile.

4 Back-butter the new tile (see page 64) with mastic or ready-mixed adhesive and press it into place. Wipe away the excess mastic. Grout the area around the tile and use your finger to push it firmly into the gap. Wipe away excess and let the grout dry. Clean up any residue with a damp sponge and apply a sealer to the new grout lines.

plastic laminate repair

Plastic laminate is a durable, long-lasting surface material as long as you take care not to cut on it with sharp knives, set hot pots or pans on it, or clean it with abrasive products. The material cannot be repaired once it is severely damaged. If a gouge goes all the way into the particle boards substrate and the substrate gets wet, the material will begin to disintegrate.

However, there are ways to repair small scratches, chips, burns, and peeling edges as well as larger damaged areas.

SCRATCHES AND CHIPS

Small scratches can be disguised temporarily with countertop polish. You will need to reapply it every few months. Or you can rub a small amount of plastic seam filler (available through the plastic laminate manufacturer) into the scratch and then remove any excess with solvent.

Larger chips, up to ¼ inch, can be repaired with laminate-repair paste. It comes in a limited range of standard colors or can be matched to the color of your countertop. Before applying the paste, wipe the damaged area clean with the solvent recommended by the manufacturer. Then squeeze a small amount onto a piece of scrap laminate or plastic and stir it with a polished putty knife to thicken it.

Apply the paste to the damaged area and spread it with the putty knife. Let it dry for the recommended time and then clean the surrounding area with solvent. If the paste shrinks after it dries, repeat the process. Chips or scratches larger than ¹⁄₁₆ inch wide will need more than one application to fill.

SMALL BURNS

If a burn is light brown and does not permeate the plastic laminate, try removing it by covering it with a thick paste made of baking soda and water. Let the paste sit for up to 30 minutes and then sponge off. If the mark does not disappear, the only perfect solution is to replace either the section or the entire surface.

LOOSE EDGES

A damaged or loose laminate edge
can be removed and then replaced
with either a new strip of laminate
or a piece of wood trim. Remove
the old edge with a putty knife.
If the bond is too tight in places,
soften the glue with a heat gun
and then proceed. When the old
edging is off, sand down the
exposed countertop edge, making
sure that all old glue is removed.
Dust and clean the surface.

If you're replacing the old edge
with a new strip of laminate,
brush the edge of the plywood
with two coats of contact cement.
Brush the back of the laminate
with one coat. When the cement
is almost dry, carefully position
the strip along the edges of the
plywood and press in place. You
can also use two-part epoxy glue.
Clamp in place until it is set.

Replacing a laminate
edge can result in a
more visible seam
between the top of the
work surface and the
edge pieces. A more
attractive solution is
to replace the laminate
edge with wood trim.
Cut the trim to size
and then glue or nail
the trim to the coun-
tertop.

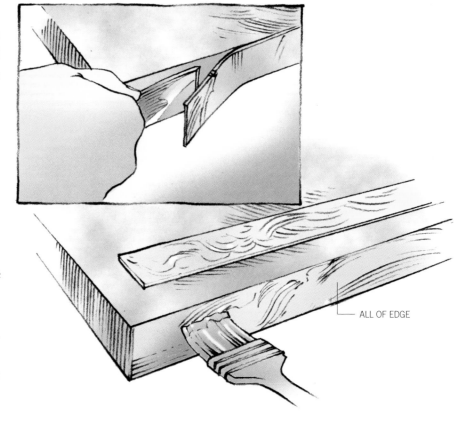

ALL OF EDGE

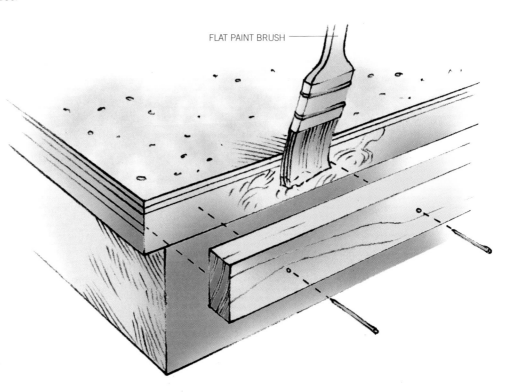

FLAT PAINT BRUSH

115

LARGER AREAS

Any large chip or burn can be cut out and replaced with a patch of new laminate. This is not a difficult process, but you do need to be sure that your cuts are precise and that you thoroughly clean the surfaces.

Another choice is to add an inlay of tempered glass cutting board called the SurfaceSaver®, made specifically for this purpose. The repair process takes some precision cutting and patience. For information on where to find this product, see the Resource Guide on page 125.

PATCHING WITH LAMINATE If you want to replace the damaged area with laminate, you need to remove only the old laminate, not the substrate. If the area is not too large, you can use a sample chip of laminate as a replacement piece. First, scribe the outline of the replacement piece onto the countertop, over the damaged area. Make sure the lines are parallel with the front edge of the countertop. Then, cut along your scribed line with a utility knife equipped with a laminate cutting blade. Use a steel square as a guide. Peel off

the old laminate and clean the substrate surface, making sure to remove all old glue.

Next, position the replacement piece or sample chip in the cutout and make sure the fit is tight and square. File edges to match the contour of the existing laminate, if necessary. When the fit is exact, apply contact cement to the substrate and to the underside of the laminate. Let dry until tacky. Then position the piece carefully in place and press to bond the two surfaces. If a seam is visible, you can use laminate-repair paste to conceal it.

INSTALLING TEMPERED GLASS A tempered-glass cutting board inlay is a great solution for repairing large areas. It comes with a metal mounting frame that sits just above the existing laminate. It will not work over a dishwasher because you have to cut through the substrate to install it. You also must be sure that the underside of the counter has a ¾-inch clearance around the cutout you will be filling.

Place the metal mounting frame on the countertop over the damaged area, with the vertical flange down. Draw a line around the outside of the flange—not along the top of the rim—and remove the frame. Make one starting hole. Then cut along the scribed line with a key-hole saw.

Next, apply caulking along the undersides of the frame on both sides of the flange. Place the frame over the glass cutting board with the textured side facing up. The punch tabs along the flange will support the glass while it is being installed. Place the cutting board and the frame in the cutout.

Then, install the lugs and bolts that come with the product. Place the plastic bolt pads over the tip of each bolt. Attach one lug close to each corner. Evenly space remaining lugs, keeping them at least 2 inches away from the weld that is midway along the back of the frame. Be sure you don't overtighten the lugs.

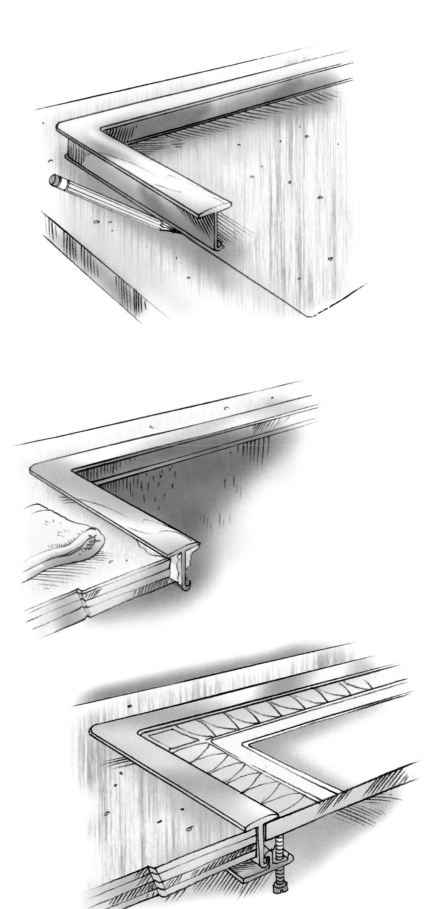

giving new life to wood tops

Wood tops are beautiful when they're well maintained, but they can be dented or gouged. Any wood top that has been finished with mineral oil or wax can be repaired with wood filler and then sanded. A butcher-block top used as a cutting surface is designed for some degree of abuse and generally requires no more than occasional sanding and a reapplication of mineral oil. Wood tops that have been varnished or painted, however, require a bit more repair.

REMOVING OLD FINISH

Before you can repair damage to a varnished or painted wood top, you need to strip away all the varnish or stain. A chemical stripper may be the most efficient way to do this. You can also sand off the finish, but this is only recommended if you have good equipment and are experienced at working with wood. Sanding is a time-consuming process, and you can do additional damage by sanding too deeply. A heat gun is another alternative. It will soften the finish so that you can scrape it off.

If you use a chemical stripper, check the label carefully to find one that is appropriate for your job. The safest

strippers do not contain the toxic chemical methylene chloride. Also look for the words "no cleanup" or "wash away with water" on the label. A "no cleanup" stripper may leave a residue, which must be sanded away. Residue from a "wash away" type can be removed by rinsing with water, but the water may raise the wood grain, making it necessary for you to sand it lightly.

Before you use a stripper, clean off dirt and scrape away loose, peeling, or flaking paint or finish.

Also round the corners of your scraping tool to prevent it from gouging the wood. Apply the

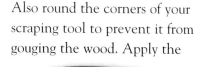

stripper as directed and allow time for it to work. Then remove the finish.

If necessary, follow up the chemical stripping by rubbing the wood with medium-grade steel wool. Soaking the steel wool in the stripper first may help remove stubborn stains. Follow the manufacturer's directions for cleaning the stripper residue from the wood. Allow the piece to dry thoroughly.

REPAIRING BLEMISHES

Once the finish is off, apply a wood filler to any damaged areas with your finger and let it dry. Apply more than one layer of filler if necessary to achieve a level surface. Sand each layer after it dries.

Sand the entire surface with 120-grit sandpaper to clean off any remaining finish and to smooth the wood. Then refine the surface with 220-grit sandpaper. Finishing sanders do particularly well at quickly achieving a uniform smoothness. Be careful to sand with the grain and apply even pressure as you sweep across the surface. Too much pressure will gouge the wood.

When the wood is smooth, clean the dust away with a tack cloth before applying a new finish. If the wood surface will be used in an area where food is prepared, protect the wood with a water-based varnish.

renewing solid-surface material

While solid-surface material can be scratched, burned, or show cut marks, it is relatively easy to restore to its original condition. Since the limited warranty refers to a manufacturer's defect, you'll need to repair minor damage yourself. If the damage is major, such as a crack, consult your supplier for options.

Small nicks, stains, and scratches on a matte or semi-gloss surface can be rubbed off with an abrasive cleaner and a scrub sponge. On a high-gloss finish, use a white polishing compound and a sponge. If that doesn't work, hand sand the damaged area. A 180- to 220-grit sandpaper is best for use on a matte finish, and a 400-grit paper is best for high gloss. Wear a dust mask and minimize dust by wetting the surface before you sand.

Once the damage is sanded away, use an abrasive cleanser to restore the finish. If the damage is still visible, use an electric sander and a heavier-grit sandpaper. Always take care to keep the acrylic dust that results from sanding from spreading.

repairing metal

Stainless steel, copper, and zinc are all durable materials. Since metal work surfaces are made by wrapping a sheet of metal around a solid substrate, such as MDF, the material should not dent easily. However, if dents do appear, they are hard to repair, so take care to avoid banging hard objects against the work surface.

Minor scratches generally add to the work surface's patina, but if they bother you, you can rub them out. Use a nonabrasive dry cleanser or a cleanser designed to clean metal surfaces in commercial kitchens and bars. You can also use metal polish. With any of these products, follow the original polishing pattern in the surface, such as a circular pattern, a half circle, or a diagonal. Identify the pattern and repeat it.

Scratches that go deeper can be removed by using a rubbing compound and the finest-grit automobile sandpaper—both are available at automobile supply stores. A wet 600-grit sanding paper works well. Start by using the rubbing compound alone, following the original pattern in the stainless steel. If this doesn't remove the scratch, wet the sand-paper and rub it lightly and slowly against the surface until you can barely see the scratch. Then reapply the rubbing compound.

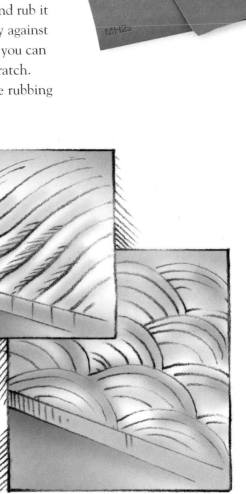

removing stains from stone

Darker stones, such as granite, slate, soapstone, and dark-colored marble, are hard to damage, especially if they've been treated with a sealer. However, stone is porous and ingredients such as red wine, vinegar, oil, and some fruits and vegetables can leave a stain, especially on lighter stones.

Stone stains because it absorbs moisture. The trick to removing a stain is to reabsorb it into a different material. There are several ways to do this. Start with the simplest, and if that method is ineffective, try another. Before using any technique, wet the area with distilled water. The stone will absorb the moisture, which will accelerate the stain-removal process.

The simplest method for minor stains is to soak the stain with an appropriate chemical agent. Let the solution sink in and then wipe the area clean with a damp cloth. If you can identify the exact cause of the stain, the chart below right will help you select the correct product for the job. If you're unsure what created the stain, you may need to test several products before you find the right one.

If a liquid stain remover does not do the trick, a tougher working solution is to use a simple poultice you make by saturating an eight-layer stack of paper towels with the chemical agent. Cover

STAIN	SOLUTION
Oil based, paint, or nail polish	First try mineral spirits, then paint remover on tougher stains
Organic (coffee, tea, fruit), ink	First try 20% hydrogen peroxide, then laundry bleach
Rust	Scrub in rust remover, then wash with household cleanser
White mineral deposits	Brush on a lime-deposit cleaner

the towels with plastic wrap and allow the paper to dry thoroughly before removing it. Wipe the area clean with a damp cloth.

A very stubborn stain may require you use a different kind of moisture-absorbing poultice, made from flour or powdered whiting, available at most paint stores.

1 Mix the dry powder with the chemical agent appropriate for the specific kind of stain. For instance, for most oil-based stains, use a poultice of 1 cup flour and 1 or 2 tablespoons of liquid dish detergent mixed with water. For wine stains, use hydrogen peroxide instead of dish detergent. The consistency of the poultice should be like peanut butter.

2 Apply the poultice ¼ inch thick over the stain, overlapping it by about an inch.

3 Cover with plastic wrap. Use masking tape to seal the edges and poke several tiny holes in the plastic to allow the poultice to dry slowly.

4 Leave the poultice in place for up to 48 hours, until the mixture is completely dry. Then scrape it away, and rinse the surface with distilled water as the last step, and buff with a soft, clean cloth. You may need to repeat the process several times before the stain is removed completely.

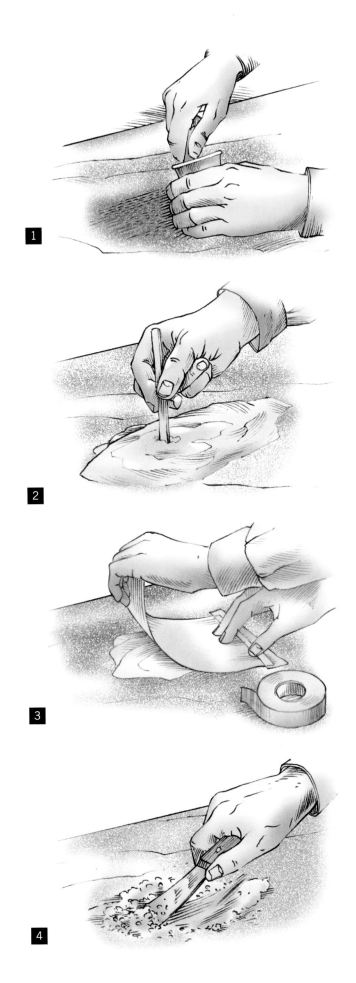

123

maintenance and care

A damp cloth and soap will usually clean any counter-top surface. When the mess is more serious and requires a little elbow grease, it's important to know which cleaning products each material can toler-ate. You should also be aware of the kind of regular maintenance your particular work surface requires to retain its original con-dition. The following chart indi-cates which products can be used on each material and notes what special care, if any, should be given.

When cleaning any surface, always remember to keep the area well ventilated when you use harsh cleaning agents such as ammonia or chlorine bleach.

MATERIAL	CLEANING PRODUCTS	SPECIAL CARE INSTRUCTIONS
Ceramic Tile	pH-neutral cleanser; solution of ¼ cup vinegar, ⅓ cup ammonia, ½ cup baking soda, 7 cups warm water	Seal grout annually; do not use abrasive cleansers
Plastic Laminate	Soap or mild household liquid detergent; car or cleaner wax for surface protection; equal parts white vinegar and water for some stains; denatured alcohol for ink stains	Do not use abrasive cleansers
Stone Tile	Stone cleaner, mild liquid dishwashing detergent, neutral cleanser	Seal annually; do not use scouring pads or products that contain lemon, vinegar, or other acids; dry with a clean towel after washing
Wood	Water (do not let stand)	Oil quarterly
Richlite	Mild soap and water; non-abrasive, non-toxic cleanser; water and vinegar	Seal with non-oil-based sealant; light scratches and burns can be refinished with a "red" scouring pad; avoid high-alkaline soaps such as dishwasher powder
Solid Surface	Soap and water, ammonia-based cleansers, commercial solid-surface cleaners	Disinfect occasionally with 1 part bleach/1 part water
Glass	Isopropyl window cleaner	Use dry cotton towel instead of paper
Engineered Stone	Soap and water, non-abrasive gel or cream cleanser, stone cleaner	
Natural Stone	Stone cleaner, mild liquid dishwashing detergent, neutral cleanser	Seal annually; do not use scouring pads or products that contain lemon, vinegar, or other acids; dry with a clean towel after washing
Stainless Steel	Any household cleanser, undiluted white vinegar, use olive oil or club soda to remove streaks	Do not use abrasive pads, cleansers, or chlorine bleach; dry with clean towel to avoid streaking
Concrete	Non-abrasive, non-acid, non-ammoniated cleanser; non-abrasive, non-toxic cleanser	Do not use abrasive pads or cleansers

...ources

...e tools and
...s shown in this
...e available through
...vement center. For
...on specific products,
... the manufacturers
...ow. When choosing
...t's best to go to a store or
...om to see the possibili-
...Most web sites can identify
...ore or dealer nearest you.

...ME CENTERS

**...owe's Home Improvement
Warehouse**
800-44-LOWES
www.lowes.com (for store location)

The Home Depot
www.homedepot.com
(for store location)

PRODUCTS

American Fiber Cement Corp.
6901 S. Pierce St., Suite 260
Littleton, CO 80128
800-688-8677
www.americanfibercement.com
SlateScape

Avonite
800-428-6648
www.avonite.com
Solid surface

John Boos & Co.
P. O. Box 609
Effingham, IL 62401
217-347-7701
www.johnboos.com
Solid butcher block

Buddy Rhodes Studio, Inc.
2130 Oakdale Ave.
San Francisco, CA 94124
877-706-5303
www.buddyrhodes.com

Caesar Stone
11830 Sheldon St.
Sun Valley, CA 91352
818-394-6000
www.caesarstoneus.com
Quartz surfaces

Cambria
866-Cambria (866-226-2742)
www.cambriaUSA.com
Quartz surface

Cheng Concrete Exchange
2808 San Pablo Ave.
Berkeley, CA 94702
510-849-3272
www.concreteexchange.com
Concrete

Crossville Ceramics Company
P. O. Box 1168
Crossville, TN 38557
931-484-2110
www.crossvilleinc.com
Stainless steel tile

Dupont Corian
800-4Corian (800-426-7426)
www.dupont.com/corian/
Solid surface and Quartz surface

Formica Corporation
800-FORMICA (800-367-6422)
www.formica.com
Plastic and metal laminate

Kampel Enterprises, Inc.
P. O. Box 157
Wellsville, PA 17365-0157
800-837-4971
Kampel SeamFil

O'BH Associates, LLC
2657 Gravel Drive, Bldg. #1
Ft. Worth, TX 76118
888-536-0042
www.formfillproducts.com
FormFill and MitreBond

Pyrolave
1817 Kenwyck Manor Way
Raleigh, NC 27612
919-788-8953
www.pyrolave.fr
Pyrolave

Richlite
624 E. 15th St.
Tacoma, WA 98421
www.richlite.com
Richlite

Schlüter-Systems L.P.
194 Pleasant Ridge Rd.
Plattsburgh, NY 12901-5841
800-472-4588
www.schluter.com
Edgings

Silestone
800-291-1311
www.silestoneusa.com
Silestone

Staron
www.staron.com
Solid surface

Vance Industries, Inc.
250 Wille Rd.
Des Plaines, IL 60018-1866
847-375-8900
www.vanceind.com
SurfaceSaver cutting board

Wilsonart International
www.wilsonart.com
Laminate and solid surface

Zodiaq
877-229-3935
www.zodiaq.com
Quartz surfaces

photography & design credits

PHOTOGRAPHERS

Ron Anderson 10 bottom left, 16 top; Scott Atkinson 86, 89, 111 bottom left, 112, 113, 114, 118, 120, 121, 122; Beateworks.com 14 bottom; Leigh Beisch 88 bottom; Wayne Cable 3 bottom, 59, 60, 63 bottom left, bottom right, 65, 69 top left; Edward Caldwell 37 bottom right; James Carrier 111 top; Todd Caverly 22 bottom; Caesar-Stone 42 bottom; 109; California Closets (©2003 California Closets Company/All Rights Reserved 128, 157; Jared Chandler 31 top; Ken Chen 52 top; Grey Crawford 25 bottom right; Jeffrey Cross 38 left; J. L. Curtis 4; davidduncan livingston.com 75 top; Frank Gaglione 108, 109; Gloria Gale 15 bottom; Tria Giovan 5 bottom left; 17 top, 20 left, 21 top, 38 right, 46, 75 bottom right; Ed Gohlich 47 bottom; Ken Gutmaker 29 bottom; Margot Hartford 30 bottom; Philip Harvey 25 bottom left, 28 top left, 30 top, 32 top, 40 top right, 51 bottom, 52 bottom, 53, 110, 119 bottom, 127; James Frederick Housel 43 top right; Jon Jensen 43 bottom; Muffy Kibbey 7, 26 top right, bottom right; David Duncan Livingston 6, 39; E. Andrew McKinney 3 middle bottom, 28 bottom, 31 bottom, 55 bottom left, 61 66, 67, 68, 69, 70, 71, 72, 73, 82, 83, 84, 85, 94, 95, 96, 97; Bradley Olman 9 top right, bottom right, 10 right, 21 middle, 23 bottom, 26 left; J. D. Peterson 43 top left; Pyrolave 49 bottom; Buddy Rhodes Studio 50 top; Richlite 36, 37 left, top right; Eric Roth Photography 2, 9 top left, 16 bottom, 17 bottom, 20 right, 35 top, 40 bottom, 41 bottom, 44 bottom, 51 top; Bill Rothschild 18, 45 bottom; Mark Rutherford 54, 55 top, 55 bottom right, 62, 63 top, 76, 77, 78, 79, 80, 81, 87, 88 top, 90, 91, 92, 93, 102, 103, 104, 105; Claudio Santini/Beateworks.com 19 top right; Michael Skott 3 middle top, 8, 13, 14 top, 15 top, 21 bottom, 22 top, 23 top, 25 top, 32 bottom; Thomas J. Story 24, 40 top left, 41 top, 42 top, 106, 107 middle, bottom; Tim Street-Porter 19 bottom left, 29 top, 33 top, 35 bottom; Tim Street-Porter/Beateworks.com 19 bottom right; Dan Stultz 28 top right, 98, 99, 100, 101; E. Spencer Toy 36 top; Roger Turk/Northlight Photography 12 top; Scott Van Dyke/Beateworks.com 50 bottom; Brian Vanden Brink 1, 3 top, 5 top, bottom right, 10 top left, 11, 33 bottom, 34, 44 top, 45 top, 47 top, 49 top, 75 bottom left; Peter Whiteley 107 top; Tom Wyatt 111 bottom right, 119 top; Eric Zapeda 48 top, bottom.

DESIGNERS

1 Mark Hutker Architects; 5 top Mark HutkerArchitects; 5 bottom right Centerbrook Architects; 7 Pamela Pennington Studios; 9 top left Louis Postel, Four Penny; 10 top left Morningstar Marble & Granite; 10 bottom left Debi Allison; 11 Peter Breese; 12 top Diane Foreman, Showplace Kitchen & Bath; 12 bottom Kitchens By Kleweno; 15 bottom Lucy St. James; 16 bottom Mark Christofi Interior Design; 17 bottom Ann Fitzgerald; 18 top The Breakfast Room; 19 bottom left Brian Murphy Architect; 20 left Tripp Hoffman; 22 top Tim Carlander; 23 top Peri Wolfman; 24 Ron Sutton, Sutton Suzuki Architects; 25 top Tom McCallum; 25 bottom right Kathleen Navarra, Navarra Consultants; 26 top right Pamela Penington Studios; 26 bottom right Ann Leanne Holder; 29 Murphy Architect; Michael Connell A top Stephen Canner 33 bottom Scholtz & Architects; 34 John Si Architect; 35 bottom Ma Lawrence Bullard Designe Martynus-Tripp Inc.; 37 bot right SKB Architects; 38 left Alan Fleming, Alan Fleming Architecture; 38 right Michae Foster 40 top right Lamperli Associates/Schlanser Design; 41 top Anne Phillips Architecture; 43 top left Nick Noyes, Nick Noyes Architecture; 43 top right J. Stephen Peterson & Associates; 44 top Elliott, Elliott, and Norelious, Architects; 45 top Io Oakes, Interior Design; 45 bottom Martin Kuckly & Associates; 46 Sherrill Canet; 47 top Sally Weston, Architect; 47 bottom Regina Kurtz, ASID; 48 Pamela Pennington Studios; 49 top Morningstar Marble & Granite; 51 bottom Steven W. Sanborn; 52 top Shari Canepa, Interior Spaces Inc. 52 bottom Architect: Frank Hennessy; Interior Design: Miller/Stein; 53 Interior Designer: Lou Ann Bauer; Contractor: Robert Roselli; 66 Heidi M Emmett; 70 Debra S. Weiss; 73 bottom left John Morris, Architects; 82 H&J Custom Woodworking; 86 Scott Atkinson; 88 Jil Peters; 89 Scott Atkinson 94 Kim Olson/K. D. Olson Construction; 98 Steve Cory; 102 Scott Atkinson; 106 Jil Peters; 108 Fred Sotcher; 125 Lighting designer: Melinda Morrison Lighting; Architects Byron Kuth, Liz Ranieri, Doug Thornley (Kuth/Ranieri).